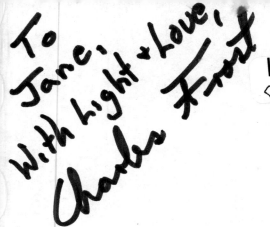

The Possible You

The Possible You

Charles Frost

BLUE DOLPHIN

Published by
Blue Dolphin Publishing, Inc.
P.O. Box 8, Nevada City, CA 95959
Web: http://www.bluedolphinpublishing.com
Orders: 1-800-643-0765

ISBN: 1-57733-023-4

Library of Congress Cataloging-in-Publication Data

Frost, Charles, 1945–
     The possible you / Charles Frost.
        p.   cm.
     ISBN 1-57733-023-4
     1. Self-actualization (Psychology)   I. Title.
     BF637.S4F76 1999
     158-dc21   98-55529
                                                                      CIP

Printed in the United States of America

10   9   8   7   6   5   4   3   2   1

Dedication

to my Mother and Father

Table of Contents

Foreword

YOU ARE HOLDING YOUR FUTURE in your hands, as you hold this book, *The Possible You.* It is a book which can help anyone desirous of experiencing a transformation in their life.

The Possible You is written with much clarity, inviting the reader to pause and reflect on the contents as they apply to them. There are exercises and numerous examples which encourage one to relate the information to their own life.

Mr. Frost has taken great care to emphasize to the reader how we create our experiences by the words we use, our predetermined attitudes and also through the dependency we have developed of relying on others' opinions and attitudes.

Unlike many books of this genre, the "how tos" are kept to a minimum, while the author does provide many opportunities for reflection. By applying the personal revelation you discover, bearing in mind that life is "choice," you are offered the opportunity of re-writing your life scenario in a manner that is fulfilling and rewarding.

Congratulations, Charles, on an offering that will be of great benefit to those who choose movement forward in their spiritual and personal growth.

Rev. Richard Ammons
Unity of Greater Lansing

Preface

IN THE 1970s I attended Fountain Street Church in Grand Rapids, Michigan. The minister, Dr. Duncan Littlefair, was a dynamic speaker and an advocate of personal change and growth as the only real and practical way to transform the world.

In the preface to his book, *The Glory Within You,* Dr. Littlefair said: "The spirit is not some thing. It is not an identifiable object. It has no independent life of its own. The spirit is not something that can be separated from the body which gives it birth and through which it expresses itself. The spirit cannot be separated from the body or saved from the body or the world. The spirit is qualitative, it is an expression of the physical. Its glory is not to save itself from the world or the body, but rather to redeem the body and the world. The spirit illumines the world, lights up the darkness of mere matter. The spirit gives meaning, purpose, dignity, and worth to an otherwise senseless and animal existence. The spirit is that which makes human life human and 'saves' human life. The spirit is the reason for religion and the basis of all religions, but is not something apart from the world. . . . If there is a failure in our life and religion, it is due to our having been looking for the wrong thing in the wrong place and missing the glory that was all about us waiting to be revealed by the light of our understanding—the light of the spirit."

Dr. Littlefair wrote and preached that the glory was within us; that if there was to be any real change in the world, it must start within each individual.

I have not forgotten.

In 1976, my former wife and I were married by Dr. Littlefair. In 1980, we moved to Texas, and, in 1987, we divorced. I was crushed. I knew Life didn't work and the divorce just assisted me in my knowledge of my failure as a person. I was sure my world had fallen apart.

As I often say in the workshops: "I went through the big D, the divorce, and went into the big T, therapy." The type of therapy I went through and later became certified in was Neuro-Linguistic Programming (N.L.P.) Briefly stated, I define Neuro-Linguistics as the theoretical study of the effect of language on the nervous system. Thus, what we say, how we say it, and how we structure the words are all clues into the Belief System, and if we can understand how this information is structured, we can use it to assist ourselves in the change process—if we choose to change.

After my certification, I was asked to do some counselling by a local church. The people I was counselling started to change, and, in 1988, I was asked to teach a class on my theories of change and growth. From that original class, there evolved a series of workshops known as Nurturing Life Process. These workshops, like Life itself, have been a process of evolution, and this book is an outgrowth of them. I did not set out to write *The Possible You*, yet it is a logical extension of the workshops and a way of teaching a much broader audience.

I believe Life is a process and we are able to change and grow, and we can each express the glory within us.

Thanks, Duncan.

I would like to acknowledge Sherry Sheffield, master N.L.P. practitioner, for her guidance in my training and her on-going support since. I would also like to acknowledge Juanita Hold-craft who found me doing workshops and referred me to people who she thought might be interested in what I was doing. And I extend a very special thank you to Rev. Bill King and Rev. Linda Pendergrass for their support and encouragement when I was first starting out. Finally, and perhaps most importantly, I would like to acknowledge all the people I've met across the United States who have shared their experiences with me.

To all of you, God bless you. This book is for you.

1

Perceptual Reality and the Possible You

THE PROBLEM WITH BELIEF SYSTEMS is that we believe them, and, more often than not, we are unaware of where any given Belief comes from or how we got it. To illustrate this, please consider a story: The Saga of the Boneless Ham.

A man and his wife have their three grown children in for Easter dinner. Every year, they have a large boneless ham as part of this dinner. This year, the man is in the kitchen helping prepare the meat, and he notices his wife cuts off both ends of the ham before she cooks it. One quarter of the ham is in the trash before it is ever cooked.

After the meal is over, the kids are gone, and they are cleaning up, he turns to his wife and asks, "Honey, how come you cut off both ends of the ham and threw them out before you cooked it?"

She stops . . . pauses . . . and ponders on it for a few moments, before she answers, "Well, that's the way my Mother always did it."

At Thanksgiving, they have dinner at her Mother's, and there on the table is a large turkey, and a big boneless ham, with both ends cut off.

After the meal, he goes up to his Mother-in-law and asks, "Mother, how come you cut off both ends of the boneless ham before you cooked it?"

She stops . . . pauses . . . and thinks about it for a minute or two, and answers, "Well, that's the way my Mother always did it."

Well, Grandma is still alive, and she's a modern kind of lady. She has her own condo in Vero Beach, Florida, and she has the whole family in every year between Christmas and New Year's. And, there on the table is a gigantic roast beef, a huge turkey, and a large boneless ham, with both ends cut off.

Later, he goes up to her and asks, "Grandma, how come you cut off both ends of the boneless ham before you cooked it?"

Without a moment's hesitation, she answers, "It's the only way it fits in the pan."

The point of this story is much of what we learn, we learn indirectly, without really knowing the reason we are doing what we are doing. When we are young, messages are sent, messages are received, and we are totally unaware of either happening. The result is we often end up with Beliefs which we have no idea of the concept behind.

What makes this even harder to deal with is the fact that most people have a Belief System in place by the time they turn five years old. Adler takes it even further by stating most people never change their Belief System once they get; they only adapt it to different circumstances This means most of us are walking around with Belief Systems we got twenty, thirty, or more years ago.

Is this the way we want to spend the rest of out lives?

And what is the Belief most of us emerge with?

Most of us don't believe Life works or that we can lead out lives in a personally fulfilling and meaningful manner to ourselves as individuals. I know this is a strange statement to make at the start of a book on possibility thinking, yet I've found it to be true. Most of us, however, somehow, sometime, somewhere along the way learned Life didn't work and that we didn't have the right to lead out lives in a personally fulfilling and meaningful manner to us as individuals.

It isn't true, and yet most of us feel this way. This is the Reality most of us live with most of the time.

I contend Life works perfectly well at every moment in time and the primary way it works is through what I call The Flow Chart of Life.

The Flow Chart of Life

The Flow Chart of Life is the way I believe life works. We start with something called FACT. A fact is a fact is a fact. I believe a FACT can be defined as something which can be described in descriptive terms without any personal interpretation. A Fact is merely what happened, or what is happening.

FACT: I am wearing deck shoes with a suit and tie.

Following FACT is PERCEPTION.

FACT   PERCEPTION

Perception is how we Perceive the Fact. Perception is what we think, and what we feel, about the Fact.

Here are two Perceptions about wearing deck shoes with a suit and tie:

PERCEPTION NUMBER ONE: I have absolutely no fashion sense and rotten self-esteem if I wear deck shoes with a suit and tie. Doing so, detracts from my workshops and invalidates what I am saying.

PERCEPTION NUMBER TWO: I must have the most self-esteem and self-confidence in the world to be wearing deck shoes with a suit and tie.

Believe it or not, I have heard both Perceptions as a result of wearing deck shoes. Each is a Perception of the exact same Fact, and yet the conclusions could not be further apart. And, because neither person bothered to ask any questions about what they were observing, neither found the reason behind my wearing deck shoes. I have a very painful foot and back condition which is aggravated when I stand on my feet for extended periods of time. It is for this reason I almost always wear either deck shoes or tennis shoes. This has nothing to do with "self-esteem" and everything to do with taking care of myself, making choices which honor and nurture myself.

FACT/PERCEPTION EXAMPLE NUMBER TWO:

FACT: Presently, about half of my workshops are attended by less than 20 people.

PERCEPTION NUMBER ONE: Oh, wow, am I ever bummed out. Anything less than 20 people just isn't worth my time.

PERCEPTION NUMBER TWO: Hey! Are we gonna have a good time or what?

Guess which Perception I have.

The result of PERCEPTION is BELIEF. Belief is what we believe as a result of what we have Perceived about the Facts. Belief is what we believe as a result of what we think, and what we feel, about the Facts. In other words, our Beliefs are coming to us through a window, or a FILTER, called PERCEPTION.

FACT   PERCEPTION   BELIEF

If we are paying very close attention to this structure, we may have just noticed our Beliefs are two steps removed from the Facts, rather than being one and the same. And, if we were willing to allow ourselves to Perceive differently, we would have different Beliefs.

The final step in the Flow Chart of Life is BEHAVIOR.

FACT   PERCEPTION   BELIEF   BEHAVIOR

BEHAVIOR is how we act and react to and with other people as a result of what we believe as a result of our Perception of the Facts. Behavior is how we act and react towards ourselves, how we treat ourselves, as a result of what we believe as a result of what we Perceive about the Facts.

Most Behavior is predictable. If we understand another person's Belief System, we can predict what their Behavior will be in most circumstance.

A good example of this is "button pushing."

All button pushing is, is a straight A B transaction. Someone wants a certain Behavior (B) from us. This person has noticed that when they treat us a certain way, when they hold themselves a certain way in relationship to us, when they speak to us in a certain way, or use certain words, or say specific things to us, we react in a certain manner. They have discovered their action (A) results in our Behavior (B). Either knowingly, or unknowingly, they have accessed our Belief System and are using this information to bring about the desired reaction.

What if we could react in other way?

What if we could adopt new Behavior?

What if we could change every Belief, and every Behavior, we have in our lives?

It's possible.

And, for most of us, it's almost totally impossible.

We have become almost completely entrenched in our Belief system and find change and growth as threatening. We are sure our Beliefs are correct, the world is the way we believe it to be, and that is just the way things are. Thus, our Beliefs, and our Reality, have become one and the same, and we are caught in a continual loop of Belief and Behavior.

In fact, this dynamic points out one of the reasons real, meaningful change is so hard to bring about. Most of us are attempting to change at the point of Belief, and this is almost impossible to do.

For over 100 years, the followers of the concepts of Unity, Religious Science, Divine Science, and other branches of New Thought Christianity have been .saying, "Change your Beliefs, change your life." For 50 years, Dr. Norman Vincent Peale said, "Change your Beliefs, change your life." And every week, Rev. Bob Schuller, with the largest television audience of any religious broadcaster in the world, says, "Change your Beliefs, change your life."

Well, as some of us have noticed as we read the books, listen to the audio tapes, attend workshops and seminars, and watch the specials on PBS, we find something which seems to work great for us, and we feel really terrific, and we "change out Belief, change our life!" And for 30-60-90 days thereafter, we feel fantastic!!! Then, one day, 30-60-90 days later, we wake up and we begin to notice that the "new" Belief system looks very strangely like the "old" Belief system, and that out Behavior hardly has changed at all? Have *you* ever noticed that?

I believe the reason for this is that while "change your Belief, change your life" is true and works as far as it goes, in order for there to be any real, meaningful change in the Belief system, there must first be a change in how we Perceive ourselves. Without any real change in the Perception of who, and what, we are, and how we got this way, it is almost impossible to have any truly lasting Belief change.

Let's share some examples of Perception and Belief, and examine how they can affect our lives.

perception: "Normal"

This is the easiest, and the hardest, of all Perceptions to deal with. Most of us are not really sure what "Normal" is. Psychologists and social scientists tell us "Normal" is representative of the "norm."

The "norm" is the fiftieth percentile, the mean point in any group of numbers. It is represented by the bell curve, and the target area in the middle is the societal norm. Those areas at the far edges are where "abnormal" or "antisocial" behavior is considered to take place.

Does this definition of "Normal" make us feel better? For most of us, it does not. For most of us, this definition does not clear up anything on bring us any closer to knowing what "Normal" is.

I've had people in the workshops say: "Normal is just a setting on a washing machine," or "Normal is any thing I'm not."

Now, here is my personal definition of "Normal."

"Normal" is whatever we grew up with.

Whatever we experienced as a small child became our original contextual definition of how the world worked and of our relationship to the rest of the world. Whatever was occurring in our household of origin at a very early age became our definition of "Normal" because we didn't know things were being done differently next door, or one block away. As a small, self-referent child, our world was the house we were growing up in and whatever the significant adults modelled for us was the way we decided people were supposed to act. And every "boneless ham" was our boneless ham.

We learned our worth and relationship to the rest of the world. This became our definition of "Normal" and how the world worked.

As we grew older and began to go other places, what did we compare them to: the household of origin. We compared relationships to what we saw between the significant adults around us as children. And, when we "rebelled"—what were we rebelling against? The concept of "Normal" we grew up with. If it was not "Normal," there would be no need to "rebel" against it.

And we carry this sense of what is "Normal" and what is not into the future with us.

Please notice, I did not say it was either appropriate or productive, and it was "Normal."

Perception: Ann's 50-Year Reunion

I love the funny papers. There is so much which can be learned reading the funnies. Several years ago, the cartoon character Cathy's mother, Ann, went to her 50-year high school reunion. Once she got there, she saw two women she'd known in high school, and the following conversation took place:

> WOMEN: You were always the prettiest one in our class, Ann.
> ANN: You thought I was pretty? You snubbed me!
> WOMEN: We didn't snub you. We were just too intimidated to speak to you.
> ANN: I'VE SPENT 50 YEARS TRYING TO RECOVER FROM LOW SELF-ESTEEM BECAUSE I THOUGHT YOU WERE SNUBBING ME!!!
> WOMEN (running off): Ha-ha-ha. Isn't that silly.
> ANN (thinking): My entire life has been based on the wrong information.

What has happened here? Ann paid attention to the information one way and her friends used the information in another. Ann Perceived she was being snubbed because her friends were not talking to her, while her friends perceived Ann as being too beautiful to be spoken to.

Within each of these Perceptions is the Belief of being "not good enough." Ann was "not good enough" because people did not speak to her. The other women were "not good enough" because they were not as "beautiful" as Ann.

Each of them had a different Perception of the "Facts." Given a different Perception, everything else also changes. With this in mind, what have we been paying attention to in our lives, where does this information come from, and how have we been paying attention to it? Are there other ways in which we might view the same information, and, if so, what different Beliefs might we have as a result?

Perception: The Naughty Name

This concept was first shared with me by a minister from the greater Detroit area. I was doing a workshop on Self-Love/Self-Esteem, and he shared the following story. The stars of the story are "little Billy," age 6, and Grandpa.

GRANDPA: Billy, I know your real name.

BILLY: No you don't, Grandpa. You don't know my real name.

GRANDPA: Yes I do, Billy. I know your real name.

BILLY: No you don't, Grandpa. I'll bet you a million, zillion dollars you don't know my real name.

GRANDPA: Billy, your real name is William Henry Smith.

BILLY: (crying and upset) You know my naughty name!!

Let's stop right here and look at what's happening.

FACT: The child is 6 years old.

FACT: The child's given name is William Henry Smith.

FACT: About the only time the child hears the given name is when he has done something someone else disagrees with.

PERCEPTION: This is my "naughty" name.

Who can say what Beliefs and Behaviors are being formed out of this Perception? Or how long this Perception with affect what we do?

Consider the Fact most adults do not even use their given names in business. I contend the "naughty name" is at least part of the reason. Think of the times we have been introduced to someone for the first time and we were given their given name. We reached out to shake hands and said, "Pleased to meet you,, William."

The immediate response was, "Call me Bill."

We were introduced to the person by their given name and greeted them as such. They responded by asking us to call them by a nickname, implying a closeness and a familiarity with us which does not exist. They cannot use the "naughty name," so they use a nickname.

It is interesting to note while the nickname is also an offshoot of the given name, it is not the same as the nickname used as a child. Thus, William went from Billy as a child, to Bill as an adult, and thereby avoids using the "naughty name."

When I was in Pennsylvania, a man burst into tears at this point in a workshop. I went over and sat down next to him, asking, "What do you feel?"

He turned to me, with tears streaming down his cheeks, and said, "Oh, Charles, I'm 54 years old, and I just figured out how come I've never been able to use the name Stephen."

An Oklahoma woman shared that every time she heard the name, "Margaret," she knew her father was behind her with a belt or a board and she was going to get a beating.

A Michigan grandmother told me about her 8-year-old granddaughter. The child had always been a good student, getting As and Bs, and had never been a discipline problem. When the child entered the third grade, all this changed. Her grades suddenly dropped to Cs and Ds, and there were reports of fighting on the playground and disruption in the classroom. The parents were concerned because she had never had such problems before. The teacher, a new teacher, just out of college, was concerned because the permanent record did not show anything like this in the past. It was time for a parent-teacher conference.

The parents went first and allowed as how they did not understand why their daughter was having these problems. Nothing had changed at home: they were not fighting, the grandparents were alive, the cat, dog, and goldfish were all fine. The teacher, once again looking at the permanent record, said, "I just don't understand why Katherine Marie is having all these problems."

And the parents looked at her and responded, "Her name is Katie."

Once again, let's look at what is happening here.

FACT: The girl is eight years old.

FACT: The girl's given name is Katherine Marie.

FACT: About the only time the girl has ever heard the given name is when she has done something some significant adult disagreed with.

FACT: The teacher liked the name Katherine Marie and had used it since the first day of school.

BEHAVIOR: The little girl, age 8, was enacting the Behavior that she Believed went with her Perceived "naughty name."

As Behavior is an extension of Beliefs, the 8-year-old girl was acting out the Behavior she Perceived/Believed went with the "naughty name" she was being called by. Such powerful programming, and it was already in place at the age of 8!

Some of us did not have a naughty name. I certainty did not. I was always "Chuck" when I was growing up. I was never "Charles Henry Frost, Jr."; however, when I heard "Chuck" with a certain tonality, I knew it was time to find a hiding place until things blew over. Rather than the naughty name, I had learned the naughty tone of voice.

Like the naughty name, this tone is something we carry with us and sends us Perceptual messages. The year after my father died, I was coming through Ohio on the way to Michigan, and was on the telephone to my mother (who I call every week when I'm out on the road). Suddenly, I had that horrible sinking feeling in the pit of my stomach that I get when something is wrong. I thought to myself, "Wait a minute, this is crazy. I'm having a great month and things are going good for me, yet I feel awful. What's this all about?" Then, it hit me, and I said, "Mom, are you about to beat up on me?"

There was a stunned silence, and then she said, "Well, I was about to make some mother-like noises."

I thought about it for a .second. "Mom, look, I'm glad you're my mother. And I'm glad you're concerned about me and my welfare. I know you have learned much in 73 years that you want to share with me. And I'm glad you want to share what you know with me. But, Mom, what I want you to remember is that I'm 46 years old and that I have to base my decisions on what I think is best for me. And, Mom, while I love and respect you, I want you to know that just because you say something doesn't mean I have to do it."

"Well, maybe I should just mind my own business."

"No, Mom, that's not what I said. What I said was that you are free to tell me whatever you choose to, and what I want you to realize is that just because you say it doesn't mean I have to do it. Now, with that in mind, please go ahead and say what you have to say."

It has been very interesting since then. The conversations between my mother and I have gotten very "clean." Now, sometimes, when we are on the phone, she will say, "Oh, there I go making mother-like noises. You won't want to talk with me any more."

"No, Mom, it's okay. Just remember the usual rules are in effect. You can say whatever you want to. I'll do whatever I feel is best for me."

"Oh, I wish your brothers and sisters understood this."

Please notice. In getting this up, in making the change in how I perceived what was being said to me, I made the .situation a "win-win" by not dishonoring what my mother wants to tell me.

perception: The Report card

I would assume most of us were subjected to the ancient medieval torture known as the report card. This being so, please think back in your mind's eye to a time when we were 8, 10, or maybe 12 years old. And we just got that report card. It was the best report card we had ever had, and we were proud of it. On that report card were 3 As and 2 Bs. Maybe for some of us, it was 3 As, 1 B, and 1 C; or for the underachievers, it was 3 Bs and 2 Cs. Whatever it was, we were proud of it because our parents had made such an issue about our grades. We were proud of *that* report card and took it home and shared it with our parents right away. We wanted them to see our achievement. We wanted to hear their praise.

And, as they looked at our report card, what did we hear?

"Why do you have this C?"

"Let's get those Bs up to As."

"Why don't you do this all the time?"

Each of these answers, and many others, were a variation of "you can do better than this," which, to most of us, translated into "not good enough."

We just did out best, and it wasn't good enough.

For most of us, being "not good enough" became a way of life, the truth of our being.

As I stated before, most of us somewhere along the way made a decision that life doesn't work and we have no right to live our lives in a personally fulfilling and meaningful manner to ourselves as individuals. This is not true, yet when we are hearing endless variations of "not good enough" much of the time, it is easy to come to such a conclusion.

When I was in Montana, a woman told me she used to get all As, except for "those troublesome A-s." When .she got an A- (still an A), she was asked "What's this A- doing on your report card?" She was getting all As and she still got the message she was "not good enough."

Some of us had the misfortune to be a year or two after brother or sister who got better grades than we did. We got a double dose of "not good enough" as we often were compared by our teacher, and our parents, to the older sibling. All this did was reinforce a sense of unworthiness.

In New York, a man in his early 40s shared with me that as he entered the 8th grade his father became very concerned about his grades: "I was getting mostly Cs, with a few Bs, and an occasional D thrown in. I was used to being compared to my older sister, an all-A student. Dad just couldn't understand why my grades weren't as good as my sister's. He finally told me he knew I had the ability to do much better, and he promised me $10.00 for every marking period I brought home an all-A report card. I worked my fanny off for that first 6-week marking period. I worked the hardest I ever had, really applying myself and studying, even passing on playing football some evenings with my friends. Oh, Charles, I was *so* proud of that report card. My father looked at the card, told me A-s weren't As, and wouldn't pay me. I knew right then and there, all the work I'd done wasn't worth it. I still wasn't good enough, and, no matter what I did, I'd never be good enough. And I haven't tried since."

What a powerful message! When he was 13 he got one more "not good enough," and he quit. Now, in his 40s he still knows nothing he ever does will make any difference, so why even bother to try?

His Perception has become his Fact and he hasn't bothered to update his Belief system since he was 13. The result is a 30-year "experiential gap" because he is still using the events which occurred when he was 13 to determine his course of actions and outcomes at the age of 43. This means he has learned nothing new in 30 years!!!!

The reason this is important for each of us is that we need to be aware of the information we are paying attention to, how we are paying attention to it, and where the information comes from in the first place. If we choose not to have this awareness, change and growth become almost impossible.

When this message of "not good enough" is followed to its extreme, it becomes impossible to do anything at all in life. In Illinois, I met a man in his early 30s. He was a very intelligent person, having a double Master's Degree in Computer Science and Business Administration. He had been an outsider in high school, a member of the computer club, chess club, and rocket club. Short and wearing thick glasses, he had been considered a "brain" and was unpopular. This just served to reinforce a "not good enough" image he had from an emotionally unavailable father ("he never had anything to say") and a controlling and manipulative mother ("she never had anything nice to say"). He didn't even date until he got to college. He had married, and divorced, twice, dropped out of the business world, had his own company, closed the company, and returned to live in the basement apartment at his parent's house because he no longer could afford to live anywhere else. Further, he was afraid to go out at all. After all, he might meet somebody and they might not approve of what he was doing, or what he was wearing, or they might think he was too forward if he spoke to them. To him, the world was a fearful place.

He asked me to do some frameworking with him. I agreed.

As I said, he had been married, and divorced, twice. The first marriage was to a woman he met when they were juniors in college. She looked past the thick glasses and admired his intellect and his drive to get ahead. After graduation, they got married and she supported him while he got his double Master's Degree in only 18 months.

They were going to climb the corporate ladder together.

He was hired by a Fortune 100 company into middle management, He started at a mid-5-figure salary, car, benefits, and an expense account.

They were going to climb the corporate ladder together.

He had a solid future and would easily earn a 6-figure income within a couple of years, as well as getting profit sharing and stock options.

They were going to climb the corporate ladder together.

He was working 60, 70, 80, 90 hours a week.

And his wife ran off with his best friend because he had more time for her.

He was crushed, and decided the dream of corporate America was a lie. He quit the Fortune 100 company and formed his own computer programming company . He had the financial backing of a man he had met through his previous job and began to write, and install, his own computer programs for small and medium sized businesses.

Through one of his suppliers, he met a wonderful young woman who also did computer programming. They got married and were going to program through life together. The business grew, and he was able to spend a lot of time with his wife because they did the writing of the programs together at home. He was doing well.

His wife ran off with the financial backer because he could provide her with more things.

He was crushed: "I knew no matter what I did, it would be wrong. I knew I couldn't be good enough for anybody else, and I wasn't any good at anything. If just didn't matter, and I couldn't go on. I lost interest in the business and closed it. I wasn't good enough. It just didn't matter. Who cared? I couldn't please anybody because I wasn't good enough."

I asked him to tell me about his business.

"I was an independent computer programmer."

"Oh, okay, and how many of them are there in the United States?"

"250,000."

"And what kind of programming did you do?"

He explained and I asked, "And how many of the 250,000 independent computer programmers did this type of programming?"

"100."

"And you made a living doing this?"

"Yes."

"Well, you know, there's making a living when you're just bumping along; then there's Making a Living where you're comfortable; and then there's MAKING A LIVING!! Which of these were you doing?"

"The second one. I was comfortable."

"And how much money were you making a year?"

"I was netting $30-40,000 a year."

"Yeah, I'd call that Making a Living. Well, of the 100 others who did this type of programming, how many of them did it better than you did?"

"5."

"And you quit because you weren't good enough?"

"Yes."

"And what did you do next?"

He talked about how he drifted through some part-time jobs which he got dismissed from, how he couldn't relate to women, how he had nothing to offer anybody in a relationship, what a failure he was, and how he was afraid to speak to anybody for fear of offending them.

He knew he couldn't do anything right.

I suddenly interrupted. "Excuse me."

"Yes."

"You had your own computer programming company and were producing computer programs. Is that correct?"

"Yes."

"And there are 250,000 independent computer programers in the United States. We're talking true independents who are selling their programs to the highest bidder, custom-made programs, and don't work directly For any given company. Is that correct?"

"Yes, it is."

"And of the 250,000, 100 of them were doing the same type of programming you were doing. Is that correct?"

"Yes."

"And you earned a full-time living doing this. Is that correct?"

"Yes."

"And you quit doing it because 5 other people did it better than you did, because you weren't good enough. Is that correct?"

"Yes."

"Okay, that makes perfect sense to me. Now, could you please explain to me how it's possible you quit doing something you did better than 249,999,995 people, because the approximate population of the United States is 250,000,000 people, and, by your own admission, there are only 5 people who do it better than you. How is it possible you stopped doing something you did better than so many other people?"

He hadn't thought about it that way.

Thus, when we run into a Belief or Limitation, we might choose to ask ourselves the following questions:

1) How do I know that?
2) How do I know it is true?
3) What evidence am I paying attention to which allows me to continue to Believe like this?

Are we paying attention to what is happening in the NOW moment, or are we paying attention to something which happened years ago? Where are we drawing our sense of Self from? We may be ignoring hundreds, even thousands, of opportunities to view ourselves differently.

age 13 or age 43
WHAT ARE WE PAYING ATTENTION TO?

5 or 249,999,995
WHAT ARE WE PAYING ATTENTION TO?

One last example pertaining to "The Report Card" was given to me in Madison, Wisconsin. A woman in the audience said she never had any trouble over grades; her family wanted to know how come she could not play the piano as well as the rest of them.

Different skill, same result: "Not good enough."

Perception: The Birthday Party

In addition to the messages we have already looked over, most of us received some very powerful "not good enough" messages during the socialization process. As with the other messages, these were primarily indirect messages and we were unaware we were even receiving them. To illustrate this point, I would like to share a visualization I call "The Birthday Party."

Please go within to the quiet place within, and as you go within, breathing at your own natural breathing rate, please breath in all the possibilities you contain. And every time you exhale at your own natural breathing rate, let go of doubt, and fear, and limitation. And now, within the moment, within the possibility, within yourself, please see, or perceive, yourself as an 8-year-old child. Your best friend in the world is having a birthday party, and you are going. I want you to get in touch with the excitement you would have about going to this party. And, as you are being taken to the party by a significant adult, you get those usual parental instructions: play nice—keep your clothes clean— wash your hands before you eat—say your pleases and thank yous—don't be the first one in line—and don't take the biggest piece of cake.

Now, you are at the party, and you play, sort of, kind of, nice, and you keep your clothes semi-clean. You are called for the meal, and you go and wash your hands, and you get in line, the fifth person back. You get your food—fried chicken, hot dogs, potato salad—and you go outside to a large round table with 20 places at it. It is a beautiful sunny day, with just a few clouds and a light breeze, a perfect day for a party. And you sit in the sixth chair clockwise from the birthday person.

Now, everybody is seated, and everybody is eating, and now everybody has eaten, and the birthday cake is being brought out. Everybody is singing: "Happy birthday to you, happy birthday to you," and the candles are blown out, and taken out of the cake—and the cake is on a big platter and is cut into pieces on that platter—and on that platter, coming toward you, is the biggest piece of cake—The biggest piece of cake is right in front of you, and I want you to reach out and take the biggest piece of cake and place it on your plate—take the biggest piece of cake—TAKE THE BIGGEST PIECE OF CAKE, RIGHT NOW!!! TAKE IT AND PLACE IT ON YOUR PLATE, NOW!!!!

How do you feel?

Most people answer that they feel "guilty" or "sneaky" or "I got away with it" or "like everybody is looking at me." Each of these answers reflects a form of guilt over having taken "the biggest piece of cake." Once again, this is a "not good enough" message, and we feel guilty for having taken something we wanted.

When asked what they see the on the platter after taking the biggest piece of cake, many people will respond, "nothing" or "crumbs." In their minds, taking the biggest piece of cake equated with taking all the cake, and, thus, was "selfish" and "self-centered." Actually, there would be a number of smaller pieces left on the platter once they took "the biggest piece of cake."

Consider this, if a person is sitting in the tenth chair, and he did not see "the biggest piece of cake" taken from the platter, and is now looking at "the biggest piece of cake" (actually, it is the second biggest piece of cake) and he takes it, he also feels guilty.

And, the person sitting in the fifteenth chair did not see either the first or second biggest piece of cake being taken from the platter. As he takes the third biggest piece from the platter, he also feels guilty for taking "the biggest piece of cake."

The Fact is "the biggest piece of cake" was only a matter of Perception, and we were always able to have the biggest piece of cake. It was always all right for us to have the biggest piece of cake.

And it was always all right for us to live our lives in a personally fulfilling and meaningful manner for ourselves as individuals. Somehow, we got the message it was not, and this was never true.

Another way we "learned" this was that we were told, "Don't be selfish. Don't be self-centered." Usually, the time most of us heard this was when we were doing something by ourselves, or for ourselves. The hidden message many of us got from this experience was that we were to take care of other people, and other people's needs, before we took care of ourselves. After all, other people were more important than we were, and we learned to look out for them, often at the expense of ourselves and our own best interest.

Of course, if we are "not good enough," it makes perfect sense to try and validate ourselves through our relationships to, and with, others; and we must leave the "biggest" and "best" for them because we are not worthy of having it.

This is not true, yet we Perceived it this way, and, thus, we live our lives that way.

Staying with The Birthday Party, think about the last social or business function where there was a buffet table. At some point, the host or hostess told everybody the food was ready and to help themselves. As we look around the room, what we see is people wandering around, looking over at the buffet table, and thinking: "No sir, I can't go over there yet. There's nobody in line, and if I'm first, other people might notice and think I'm greedy and selfish."

Nobody gets in line until the host or hostess says, George," you're the guest of honor tonight. You go first." George gets in line, and, boom, the entire room is in line.

I used to live my whole life this way. Nope, I cannot be the first in line. People might think I am greedy and selfish and self-centered if I do that. I might draw attention to myself if I go first, and I cannot do that.

No longer. Now, when I hear, "Food's on," I say, "I'm there," and, boom, the whole room gets in line behind me. Are they thinking I am greedy or selfish; no, most of them are thinking, "Thank God, somebody got in line." It does not matter if I am first in line, or hundredth in line, I am going to take the same amount of food. And, if it is a really good buffet, I am going back for seconds after everybody else had been through the line the first time. This serves another useful purpose as it gives permission to those people who took those little, tiny portions to come back and get the food they really need to have a meal. The first time through, they were busy looking out for everybody else: "Got to make sure there is enough food to go around."

Once again, looking out for others before ourselves as a way of life is at work. Actually, it is the responsibility of the people giving the party to make sure there is enough food to go around, not ours. Frankly, I have seldom been to a party with a buffet table where there was not enough food to go around. Usually, there are left-overs at the end of the evening, and I hear: "Okay, who wants a whole roast chicken and a gallon of potato salad?"

Perception: The Balloon

Perhaps one of the best examples of how Perception works, and how quickly it can change, occurred when I was in South Bend, Indiana. I had given a promo for my afternoon workshop and was watching the rest of the church service. There was a segment devoted to the children, and the small children, age 3-6, came forward. The youth minister was talking about balloons, using them as an example of God's Love for all people regardless of external differences (sizes, shapes, colors). It was a terrific concept, and a basket of balloons was passed so each child could have one. In the middle of the group sat a little girl, maybe 4 years old, in a white dress and with beautiful curly blonde hair. She was so cute. As the basket came to her right, she reached out and missed the basket. It moved behind her, and she reached out, and missed again. As it came to her left, she reached out once more, and missed. She did not get a balloon. Her shoulders stumped, and her chin dropped to her chest.

While body language is not an absolute, most children do have body language which reflects what they are feeling. Based on body language, we could say, the little girl is very deep in Perception land, most likely having some deeply negative feelings about what was taking place.

I was watching. This is the type of thing I talk about. Surely, somebody else must also see what is happening, and will do something about it.

No, the presentation simply continued, and the little girl slumped more and more.

FACT: The little girl is in church, a kind, loving, nurturing environment.

FACT: Each child was intended to get a balloon (some took several).

FACT: The little girl did not get a balloon.

PERCEPTION: (based on body language) The little girl feels she is "not good enough" to have a balloon, that she is being "punished" for some reason.

Now, up to this point, the minister had thought I was a fairly normal, sane, rational human being, so imagine her surprise when she looked over and saw me leaning forward in my chair, frantically waving my arms near my legs. She looked at me quite puzzled. Noticing I had her attention, I sat back up, pointed to the children, made a stretching motion, and then assumed a slumping position.

The minister looked carefully, saw the little girl, said something to the youth minister, and the balloons were passed again. This time, the little girl took a balloon. Her entire body shifted upward and a smile lit her face.

The little girl had a whole new Perception of Reality, .and all it took was receiving a balloon.

It is sad that most of us cannot, or will not, change our Perception of ourselves as quickly as this when we receive new information. Of course, most of us are not faced with situations which are as readily correctable as this one was.

Jesus and Self-love

Many of us learned through Religion that we were not supposed to "love" ourselves. Learning, rather, that "Christian Charity" was giving to others. This only served to reinforce our feelings of being "selfish," "self-centered," and "not good enough." I believe Jesus spoke directly to this issue in Matthew 22: 34-40:

> And when the Pharisees had heard that he had put the Sadducees to silence, they were gathered together.
> Then one of them, which was a lawyer, asked him a question, tempting him, saying,
> Master, which is the great commandment in the Law?
> Jesus said unto him, Thou shall love the Lord thy God with all thy heart, and with all thy soul, and with all thy mind.

This is the first and great commandment.

And the second is like unto it, Thou shall love thy neighbor as thyself.

On these two commandments hang all the law and the prophets.

I'd like to address what Jesus said, starting with the second part, going to the first part, and then coming back to the second part. What we want to remember is Jesus said, "Thou shall love thy neighbour as thyself."

Given how most of us feel about ourselves most of the time, our neighbors could be in BIG trouble. Because if we are going to share with our neighbour the same love we have been sharing with ourselves, then out neighbor is in big trouble!!

Please notice what Jesus .said: ". . . love thy neighbor AS thyself." Jesus did not say to love thy neighbor MORE than thyself; Jesus did not say to love thy neighbor INSTEAD of thyself; and Jesus did not say to love thy neighbor AT THE EXPENSE of thyself. Jesus said to love thy neighbor AS thyself.

Thus, the quality of the Love we give unto ourselves is the quality of the Love we have to give unto others. If we do not Love, and Honor, and Nurture ourselves, it is impossible to Love, Honor, and Nurture another human being. Frankly, it is impossible to give to others that which we cannot find within ourselves first.

How important is this Love of Self? Jesus .said, "Thou shalt love the Lord thy God with all thy heart, and with all thy soul, and with all thy mind." In other words, Jesus said we are to Love God with EVERY part of our state of Beingness: our heart, our soul, and our mind. With EVERYTHING we have, we are to Love God.

Most people, regardless of how they conceive of God, can agree with this concept.

Then, Jesus built a verbal bridge when he said: " . . . the second is like unto the first," which, in modern language would translate as "The second is the same as the first." Thus, the Love which we can give unto ourselves, which is then the Love we will give unto our neighbor, is the same as the Love we will give unto God, and we will Love ourselves with all our hearts, and all our souls, and all our minds. In other words, WE WILL LOVE OURSELVES WITH EVERY OUNCE OF OUR STATE OF BEINGNESS!!!

This is not being "selfish" or "self-centered"; this is loving ourselves and then gives us a core of Love within our state of Beingness from which we may Love and Nurture other people.

Further, if as mystics and New Thought Christians believe, each human being and God meet within (the human soul), then the act of Loving and Nurturing ourselves is the act of Loving and Nurturing God.

Frankly, we can not give from an empty wagon. If we do not Love and Honor ourselves, we cannot have Love to share with other people. We cannot give to them something which we do not have ourselves!

Perception: The Dining Room Table

I grew up, as do most people, in a dysfunctional home. I allowed this to color my Self-image for many years. I was sure I had no value as a person and that anything I did in life did not matter.

I would come to the dinner table. It did not matter how old I was; I could be 6—I could be 8—I could be 10—I could even be 20 years old, and it was going to happen. I would sit down at the dinner table, the prayers were said, the food was served, and I would look up and begin to talk about what had happened to me during the course of the day, and my father would say, "Not of general interest," which meant it could not be talked about.

Now, dinner was the only time of the day that the whole family was together. This was my only chance to share what was happening to me with my mother and father and my six brothers and sisters, and it was "not of general interest." The message I was receiving from this as a 4 or 6 or 8 or 10-year-old child was: "What you say and do, what you think and feel, and what happens to you is of absolutely no interest or importance. Your life does not matter. You have no value as a person."

I took this *very* personally.

I begin to build my whole life around the Perception, and the Belief, that I had no value as a person. After all, what I had to say, and what happened to me, was "not of general interest." As I became more and more convinced that this was the Truth of my being, I built my entire sense of self-worthlessness around it and carried it with me into my early 40s.

Yet, there is another way to Perceive this, because if I take a total stranger, some human being I have never, ever met before in my entire life, and I place that total stranger at my dining room table at the age of 6, and he is now there with that relationship, to those people, at that time, in that place, and under those same conditions and circumstances, will the total stranger be treated any differently than I was?

Please notice the structure of this question: if a total stranger is placed there at the same time, in the same place, with the same relationship, to the same people, under the exact same set of conditions and circumstances, would the total stranger be treated any differently than I was?

The answer is NO! He would not have been.

Given, the total stranger may *react* differently to what happened, but if he is there at that time, in that place, with that relationship to those people, under the same set of conditions and circumstance, he will be treated exactly the same way I was because he has assumed my place in time and space. All of the factors which brought about the "not of general interest" remark remain in place, and any other person will receive the same treatment. It had nothing to do with my value as a person, and everything to do with the EXTERNAL circumstances. No matter who is there, the externals remain the same, and thus, so does the treatment.

This same principle applies to each of our lives, and no matter what has happened to any of us, it would have happened to anyone else who was there at that time, in that place, with that relationship to those people, under that set of conditions and circumstances.

Thus, IT WAS NOTHING PERSONAL!!!

Life happened live, and we were there. Film at eleven, ten Mountain and Central.

We cannot change the way other people choose to act and react. They will treat other people the same way no matter who is there at any given time under a given set of circumstances and conditions. Whatever has occurred within our lives, it was nothing personal.

> PROOF: I have 6 brothers and sisters. Each of them was also being told they were "not of general interest." (We did not "discover" this until my youngest sister was in her late 30s.) Thus, it had nothing to do with me, personally, and everything to do with my father's parenting style. He thought he was being loving and keeping control of the dinner table by not having 7 children all talking about what had happened to them individually.
>
> PROOF: My father was abrupt with any person who started talking about something my father was not interested in personally.

"Not of general interest." It was not just me. It was anything he was not interested in. And, it was nothing personal. He was just busy being who, and what, he was.

In all of this discussion of Life being nothing personal, there are two things I have NOT said which are equally as important as what I have said.

1) I did not say that what happened to us did not happen. It certainly did happen, and we certainly were there. And it was nothing personal.

denial

2) I did not say that what happened to us was either appropriate or productive, and I did not say we had to approve of what had happened. I said it was <u>nothing personal.</u>

Certainly, many of us have had things happen in our lives which were neither appropriate or productive: we were abused emotionally and physiologically; we were physically battered and beaten; we were verbally abused; we were sexually abused and molested. It happened. We were there. We felt the fear, the pain, the sense of self-loathing.

denial

And it was <u>nothing personal.</u> It would have happened to anybody else who had been there at that moment in time, in that place, with that relationship to those people, under that set of conditions and circumstances.

With this being so, how is it possible we have chosen to build our entire lives and self-images around such events? How is it possible we have decided to endlessly relive some thing which occurred many years ago rather than to live in the present and get on with the rest of our lives? As long as we choose to see this event, or events, as the measuring stick for our lives, we are trapped in the past and have no real chance of changing our Beliefs, or our lives, and it is all based on the Perception that Life somehow singled us out in some manner, and that whatever happened to us is who, and what, we are.

As long as we view it this way, we are right, and our lives will never change. We will be trapped by our past, and by our Perceptions of the past, and our lives will endlessly repeat the same types of things over and over again until we choose to let go of the past and begin to live the rest of our lives based on different information.

A wonderful example of this concept is the main character in the movie, *Groundhog Day.* He literally was reliving the same day over and over and over again until he came to understand it was not how others treated him, but it was how he REACTED to others which made the difference in how his life worked.

While most or us do not actually continually relive the same day, we often do so in a figurative sense until we decide to let go of the past and do things differently.

Another example of this is the story about the person who lived in an apartment building downtown and walked to work every day. On day, he came out of his building, turned right at the corner as he always had done, and half way down the block, he fell into this big hole. It took him all day to get back out of the hole. He went home. Cleaned up. Went to bed. The next morning he got up and was going to work. He took a right at the corner, and half way down the block, he fell into the big hole again. It took him all day to climb back out of that hole and he missed another day of work. He went home. Cleaned up. Went to bed. The next morning he got up to go to work. He took a right at the corner, and half way down the block, he fell into the same big hole again. It took him all day to climb out of the hole and he missed a third day of work. He went home. Cleaned up. Went to bed. The next morning he got up, got ready for work, left the building, crossed the street, and went on to work. He finally realized that if he did things just a bit differently, he could have different outcomes in his life.

It is not so much the FACTS, or our BELIEFS, which have limited us. It has been the PERCEPTION of the FACTS which created our BELIEFS which has limited us. If we will allow ourselves to PERCEIVE ourselves, and our lives, differently, then everything else will start to change.

The Reasons We Don't Change

Far too often, even knowing all this, we will not change. In most cases, it is because we do not want to change. We have an investment in keeping things a certain way, viewing the world and other people a certain way, and if we were to allow these things to change, it would, in our opinion, make the past and everything we know pointless and meaningless.

When this is so, we develop a resistance to change.

The way we view change is: if I change, it is an admission that I was wrong in the past. It would be saying I did things wrong in the past.

In short, we "beat up" on ourselves.

Change is our enemy.

We view change as just another way of being told we are "not good enough." We were "not good enough" in the past, and we need to do "better." Given this viewpoint, it is no wonder change and personal growth are so hard to achieve.

This happens because we are taking what we are learning here in the NOW moment, and we are retroactively applying this information to events which happened in the PAST. We are using new information and skills as a way of proving we were "not good enough" in the PAST because we did not know then what we do know now.

"I don't want to change because it shows me what I did wrong in the past. I don't want to change because it points out my past failures when I didn't know about this."

Excuse me, it is time for a very serious REALITY CHECK: We did not know what we knew before we knew it, so how is it possible to apply it to something which happened in the past?

Using such illogical logic can keep us forever trapped in a continual loop of never being good enough. There will be something new we learn tomorrow, which makes what we know today, "not good enough."

I could use such logic this way: "If I were to take the skills, abilities, and resources I presently have, my knowledge of those skills, abilities, and resources, and my opportunity to use them, back in time to a year or two before my divorce, I could save my marriage!" How stupid could I have been not to use then what I have now? This, of course, also means that the skills, abilities,

"inertia"

and resources I had available to me then were "not good enough" and what I did then was "not good enough"—based on what I know today.

The challenge with such logic is that I developed the skills, abilities, and resources I have available to me today as a result of, not in spite of, the divorce. I do not get here without having been there.

I contend change is the natural outgrowth of life, and that there is no such thing as Failure. There is only Feedback, another opportunity to learn. It is all in how we view it. We can have Failure in our lives, or we can have Learning Opportunities.

Perhaps one of the best stories illustrating this point is about Thomas Edison. It took Edison 10,001 attempts to invent the light bulb. It was the 10,001st time when he got his working model. Shortly thereafter, a reporter asked him, "Mr. Edison, how did it feel to fail 10,000 times?"

Edison responded, "Son, I never failed. I had 10,000 chances to learn something new. Every time I was able to learn something new which I could apply to the next attempt."

What a wonderful attitude!

Most of us were far more persistent as children when we were learning to ride a bicycle or skate than we are as adults. When we were children, every time we fell down, we got back up and kept going until we mastered the skill we wanted to learn.

As an adult, most of us seldom do so. We are afraid of looking silly or stupid the first time we do something. We are afraid of what other people will think of us. We quit right away if we feel we are not getting the maximum desired result at once. We did not get it "right," so we turn and walk away, a "failure" once again.

The fact was it was all in how we Perceived it.

[handwritten margin note: about as accurate as Newton and the apple (i.e., not very)]

FAILURE OR FEEDBACK?
WHAT DO WE WANT?

FAILURE OR LEARNING OPPORTUNITIES?
WHAT DO WE WANT?

Given, some learning opportunities will be more optimum than others; however, if we are "learning," it is impossible to fail. In order to FAIL, we must reach an outcome past which nothing will ever happen, and past which nothing will ever change. If we are allowing ourselves to "learn," and "change," and "grow" from what is taking place in our lives, there are no "final" outcomes, no end points, and we can not fail at anything.

The Security Freak

Still, many of us "fail" to the extent that we are attached to achieving given, specific results. Having observed such behavior in myself and others, I arrived at this definition of a Security Freak.

A SECURITY FREAK is a person who wants to know what the end result is before they will ever undertake the initial action. Internally, the Security Freak is saying, "You tell me how it will come out, and then maybe I will do it," or "I will tell you I love you after you have told me that you love me." The Security Freak wants a sure thing.

I spent most of my life being a Security Freak. I had a manufacturer's rep company (independent salesman working on commission). I was on a draw against commission and getting a monthly, or quarterly, bonus with every company I represented. I would wake up in the morning, and I was already making money. Somebody, somewhere, was ordering something. It was great! It was a Security Freak's dream!! Then, I closed the sales business to go out and do workshops and seminars throughout the United States, under the following terms and conditions:

1) I pay my own expenses, accepting housing when it is available;
2) I do not ask for a financial minimum; and,
3) I split the workshop receipts with the sponsoring church or organization.

To the Security Freak, such an arrangement cannot work; however, it has worked perfectly well for me. The old Security Freak part of me screams out, "It might not work. There might be lack. What will you do it nobody shows up?"

And I have never lacked the resources to do what had to be done or to get from one place to the next.

Lack Thinking

The Security Freak is an example of lack thinking. When we are in Lack Thinking, we think: "If I do not have certain things, or if things do not go a certain way, it will not work."

Out of this type of thinking, we come to know that there is one thing which is more important than anything else in the entire world, and if we do not have it, if we can not keep it and possess, if we do not have it with us at every moment in time, we are insufficient as individuals and our lives do not work.

I got lucky. I found the secret of Life in Kenosha, Wisconsin, in July, 1991. I found THE ONE THING I know I must have in order for my life to work and for me to be all right as an individual. I have kept it with me, safety placed in a cash box, ever since.

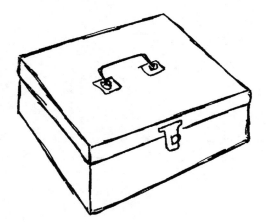

I know if I do not keep what is in this cash box to myself, if I don't hide it, and protect it, and make sure it is always there, my life will not work and I will be incomplete as an individual.

"hoard"

Yes, without this particular packet of grape jelly, my life will not work and I will be lost as a person. If I do not have, and keep, this particular packet of grape jelly, if I do not ~~horde~~ it, and protect it, and never let it out of my sight, I will never have any grape jelly.

That is it.

That is all there is.

There is not any more.

Now, the challenge, or the opportunity, with this line of thinking is that grape jelly comes in many sizes:

and grape jelly comes in many shapes:

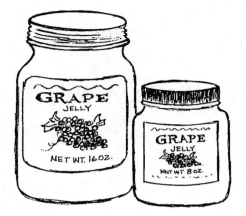

in fact, there is an abundance of grape jelly:

and we have turned it into this:

We have taken a single person, and turned that person into our sense of Love and Loveability. If the person I Love does not Love me back, there is no Love. If the person I Love does not Love me in the manner I want to be Loved, I am not Lovable.

We have taken a job, or a certain income level, and turned that into our sense of prosperity and abundance.

To the extent we allow ourselves to do this, we create lack and limitation in our lives. Because we have already determined what the end result is supposed to be before we ever take an action, we limit the results we can achieve. We settle for the single packet of grape jelly when the Universe has an abundance of grape jelly available to us for every area of our lives.

Still, if, we are "loved" by a certain person, or in a certain way, or if our "prosperity" does not come from a certain source and at a certain time, we feel a sense of Lack.

It is not true, yet it is the way we view it. We have cut ourselves off from the natural abundance of Love which is the Truth of God and of the Universe.

I call this THE GRAPE JELLY PRINCIPLE OF LIFE.

WHAT DO WE WANT?

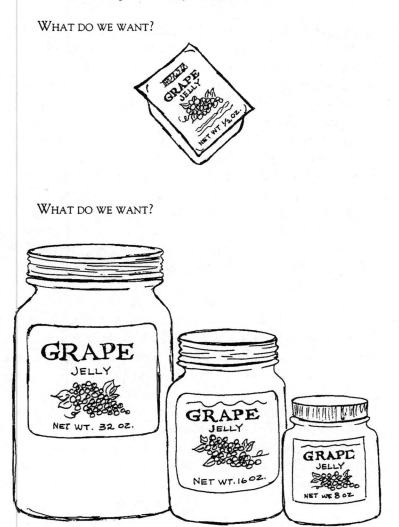

WHAT DO WE WANT?

It is a choice we have to make.

And our sense of lack will exist to the extent we pay attention to the single packet of grape jelly rather than the natural abundance of the Universe which is all around us.

I remember the first year I was out doing workshops full time. I had created several learning opportunities for myself. I started during the summer, which is, perhaps, the single worst time to present workshops, as people are on vacation and doing summer activities. I had only scheduled one or two workshops per week; certainly not enough to provide the financial resources needed to stay on the road and also pay the on-going bills from home. And I was doing the best I knew how to do at that time; the new information allowed me to adjust what I did in the future.

I had an old friend in Grand Rapids who had told me I could use the spare bedroom of his condo as my "home base" while I was in the Great Lakes area. Towards the end of the third week, as I was coming in one night, he said to me: "Chuck, we have to talk. This just isn't going to work. You have to find another place to stay."

I had no idea what this was about. I had been out of town far more than I had been in town. I was getting up before he did in the morning and going out for breakfast. I was not using his phone. I was usually coming "home" late in the evening after having been with other friends and/or family.

What I did know was that something about my being there was "triggering" something from his past, and that any attempt to discuss this would be taken as an argument, only further straining the situation. (As it turned out, this was correct. He had allowed some friends who were in recovery to stay in the past. They had run up his phone bill and eaten his food without asking. As my staying there acted as an "echo" to those events, and he was paying attention to the past rather than the present, I had to go.)

I told him I would move as soon as possible, and that night as I lay in bed I said, "Okay, God, if this is what you want me to do, I need a place to live."

Three days later, when I was in South Bend, Indiana.. I went to dinner after my workshop with some people I had met while presenting at a retreat. They asked me how things were working out, and I told them about what had happened. They offered me the use of a fishing cabin they owned if I would just pay the utilities for the time I was there. The cabin had no hot water, no shower, and no telephone, and it was perfect for my usage. I stayed there for 10 weeks, paying only the utilities.

Prosperity was not a cash amount. It was a place to live.

Another time, I was in Pennsylvania. I was the guest speaker and did a workshop at a church in Harrisburg on Sunday. Monday, I had gone to Gettysburg to tour the area. Tuesday, I drove up to Wilkes-Barrie where I was presenting a workshop Wednesday night. When I arrived at the church, the minister was busy. I was given a desk to work at as I had phone calls to make, regarding future workshops elsewhere in the country. Several hours later, we were both done, and she asked me if I would like to go to dinner with her. I said yes, and was to follow her. I went outside, started the car, put the car in gear, and pushed the brake pedal all the way to the floor.

I carefully followed her. When we sat down, I told her what had happened. It turned out that her husband was a master diesel mechanic and had his own rebuilding facility. After dinner, we carefully took my car there and left it. I took what I would need for the night with me.

The following morning, while we were having coffee, her husband called: "You tell Charles there is no way he came over the mountains in that car. The right-hand brake line is shattered. The left-hand brake line is cracked. There is no brake fluid. The brake pads are completely shot and need to be replaced. His car is a torpedo."

Yet, it had carried me across the mountains and to the church, only going out once I was there. He repaired the brake for me as a "gift" in return for the work I was doing for others.

Prosperity was not a cash amount. It was the car brakes.

And take one more look at the conditions under which I do a workshop. I do not ask for any minimum or financial guarantee. Even given that, let's say I had the Perception mentioned earlier: anything less than 20 people does not work. IF I BELIEVE THAT, THEN ANY TIME I GIVE A WORKSHOP TO LESS THAN 20 PEOPLE, I FAIL BEFORE I EVER OPEN MY MOUTH!!

How often are we doing this to ourselves in life? How many times are we creating Failure for ourselves, rather than accepting we have achieved a result and can use this new information to move into the Future?

It is all in how we Perceive it!!

Once we understand this, we can use the Flow Chart of Life and the concept of Perceptual Reality to assist us in making changes in every area of our lives.

2

Language and the Possible You

LANGUAGE IS A POWERFUL TOOL through which we communicate with both ourselves and others. How we choose to
represent ourselves verbally reflects how we view ourselves, the
world about us, and our value in the world. Whatever we are
doing linguistically shows up also in our Belief system. As I have
already asked, do we want "Failure" or "Learning Experiences"?

Some people might say this is "splitting hairs" or "playing
word games," and, I suppose that is one way to view this.
However, think back to the number of times we were feeling
really great and then somebody said something which brought us
down, upset us, or made us angry. The question becomes: was it
what was said which made us feel this way, or was it how we
Perceived what was said which made us feel this way.

Again, my personal definition of Neuro-Linguistics ad-
dresses this: "Neuro Linguistic Programming is the theoretical
study of the effect of language on the nervous system. Hence,
what we say, how we say it, the words that we choose, and how
we structure those words are all clues into the Belief System. If
we understand this information, we can use it in the change
process—if we choose to change."

47

With this in mind, I would like to address some specific language patterns which I believe can limit our possibilities.

Why Not "Why?"

Of all the language patterns commonly used, I believe the single most dangerous and counterproductive to good, productive conversation is the question, "Why?"

There are three major reasons I make this statement:

1) "Why?" is an assumed attack statement to most people. The person receiving a "why" question will feel they are being attacked.

2) For most people, "why?" assigns blame, guilt, and shame. If the person receiving the question is already feeling blame, guilt, and shame, they will go deeper into the feeling, and communication will become more difficult.

3) Because "why?" is an assumed attack statement and assigns blame, guilt, and shame, we probably receive a lot of non-useful information in return. If a person feels he is being "blamed" for something, he will try to "defend" himself, whether or not such defense is necessary. We will receive excuses and rationalizations for what has happened, not the reasons for what occurred.

How much more productive would it be if we were to ask other people "How is it possible?" rather than "Why?" "How is it possible?" is not a perceived attack statement, is not emotionally loaded, and usually results in our receiving the information we were looking for, the reasons behind whatever occurred.

In almost every workshop, somebody will point out most children seem to use the word, "why?" naturally. I then ask where they are getting it from. For most, it went something like this:

Why did you open the cupboard and pull out all the pots and pans? Why did you spray whipped cream all over the kitchen? Why did you hit your brother/sister? Why did you pull the cat's tail? Why did you run out in the street after I told you not to?

Children learn their language patterns from the adults around them. If we change our language patterns, and thus, how we Perceive and represent ourselves to the world, we will also begin to change the language patterns of any children who are in the household.

I did some counselling for a young married couple a few years ago. They were having some serious problems and came to me after being referred by a friend. In the first session, I had them talk with each other about the problems and difficulties they were having. They talked for about an hour and a half before I stopped them. They looked at me with an "okay, now fix us" look. I told them I had heard them ask many "why?" questions to each other and that they actually had argued after such a question. I then explained the Why?/How Is It Possible? framework and told them I wanted them to use "How Is It Possible?" rather than "Why?" when talking with each other, and even when they were "talking" to themselves, over the next few weeks.

In a follow-up visit three weeks later, each of them remarked on how they felt the quality of their communication with each other had improved, and that they were talking more, arguing less.

They had a 2-year-old son. He is now in grade school, and loves to follow his dad around the house when his dad is doing things. When his dad does something he doesn't understand, he asks, "Hey, Dad, how is it possible. . . ?" Because he was exposed to this framework, he now uses it, and he lives in a world filled with Possibility rather than blame, guilt, and shame.

This is important to recognize because 80-90% OF ALL THE CONVERSATIONS WE HAVE IN LIFE ARE INTERNAL. WHATEVER LANGUAGE PATTERNS WE ARE USING EXTERNALLY, WE ARE ALSO USING

INTERNALLY ON OURSELVES. We are constantly talking to ourselves, and most of us are "whying?" ourselves to death, preventing ourselves from reaching a more positive and productive state of mind.

"Try"

The word, "try" is, I believe, the second most counter-productive word in the English language. Do we "try" to pick up a pencil? Do we "try" to have a drink of water?

No, of course not. We picked up the pencil, and we had the drink of water. We completed an action.

"Trying" is another way we set ourselves up for Failure. When we have something to do, we either do it, or we do not do it. There is no such thing as "trying."

The way I like to make this point in workshops is to have somebody stand about 5 feet from me. I tell them, "Now, without moving from that spot, and without leaning, I want you to try and touch me." Usually, the subject will look at me like I have lost my mind. I have given them an impossible task. Actually, all I have done is established the boundaries beyond which the person can not go, pre-establishing how it will work. At this point, I tell the subject to cancel everything I have previously said and just step forward and touch me. The subject steps forward and touches me.

Can we understand the difference? When we say, "I'll try," we have already established how it will not work. Think about it. When we hear other people use the word, "try," it usually goes something like this: "I'll try, but it just won't work." "I'll try, but it won't happen." "I'm trying as hard as I can."

"Try" to get up out of your present seat. We either can do it, or not. We can either stand up, or not. DO NOT TRY, JUST DO IT!!! WHATEVER HAPPENS IS A RESULT, AND WE CAN NOW MOVE FORWARD BASED ON THE NEW INFORMATION WE HAVE RECEIVED!!

"Should"

Many people consider "should" (along with "would" and "could") as the most counter-productive word in the English language. I agree "should" is counter-productive, and place it in third on my personal list. Here are two examples of how "should" can affect us.

"I Should" Part I

Charles: I want you to tell me something you feel you should do.

Subject: I should be looking for a job more seriously than I am right now.

Charles: Who said you should?

Subject: I did.

Charles: Before you, who said you should be looking harder for a job than you are right now?

Subject: A number of different people.

Charles: Who, specifically?

Subject: Don.

Charles: Before Don, who said you should be looking harder for a job than you are right now?

Subject: Ralph.

Charles: How do Don and Ralph know what you should do?

Subject: They both have jobs.

Charles: How do they know what you should do?

Subject: Because they are just trying to be helpful.

Charles: Okay, and before Don and Ralph, who said you should be more serious about looking for work than you are now?

Subject: This is in the past.

Charles: That's fine. This is the reason we stay in the present and work the chain backward.

Subject: My father?

Charles: And before your father said you should try hard to be
employed, who said you should?

Subject: Nobody.

Charles: How do you feel about the fact your father said you
should be employed?

Subject: I don't know.

Charles: And how do you feel about that? How does he know
what you should do?

Subject: I don't think he does.

Charles: How do you feel about the fact you are unable to do
what you should do?

Subject: Not too good.

Charles: Not too good?

Subject: Good, now that I understand where the feeling comes
from, I can deal with it.

What we can notice here is the "root" of the "should" is
something which the subject heard from a significant adult when
the subject was a child. The fact is, most of the "shoulds" we find
in our lives come from something we originally were told when
we were children. As we can see in this example, the "should"
can be traced back to an authority figure, in this case the father,
and we begin to think: "Well, my father may not always know
what is best, but he says I should do this and he's right!" A
message such as this can bring us to an important ecology check
of who the significant adults were when we were growing up and
what messages they might have given to us. To see how these
messages and the resulting Belief and Behavior pattern can
cripple a person and assist in bringing about additional non-
functional patterns and feelings of negative self-worth, look at
what transpires in the following example.

"I Should" Part 2

Charles: I want you to tell me something you think you should do.

Subject: I should have my own business.

Charles: Who said you should have your own business?

Subject: I do.

Charles: Before you said you should have your own business, who said you should?

Subject: My mother and my spouse.

Charles: And before your mother and your spouse, who said you should have your own business?

Subject: Almost everybody.

Charles: Who is almost everybody?

Subject: Most of my friends.

Charles: How do they know what you should do?

Subject: Oh. They don't. They can't.

Charles: Before your friends, who said you should have your own business?

Subject: I guess my spouse did.

Charles: How does your spouse know what you should do?

Subject: She doesn't, but she knows I want to have my own business.

Charles: What's important about having your own business?

Subject: You have your own money, and you can do the things you want to do when you want to do them and you don't have to worry about it. You don't have to worry about money. People know you are a success, that you have done something with your life.

Charles: If you have your own business, you are a success?

Subject: Yes.

Charles: So, is this about having your own business, or is this about being a success?

Subject: It is about being a success.

Charles: And who said you should be a success.

Subject: My father.

Charles: Did your father say you should have your own business?

Subject: Yes.

Charles: And this was before you thought, or said, you should have your own business?

Subject: Yes.

Charles: And did your father tell you that you would be a success if you had your own business?

Subject: Yes.

Charles: How does your father know you will be a success if you have your own business?

Subject: Well, he has his own business.

Charles: Where?

Subject: In Florida.

Charles: Did he ever have a business here?

Subject: Yes.

Charles: Is that the business he has in Florida?

Subject: No.

Charles: What happened to the business he had here?

Subject: It went out of business.

Charles: How did it go out of business?

Subject: It went bankrupt.

Charles: Your father had a business which went bankrupt?

Subject: Yes.

Charles: And your father says you are a success if you have your own business?

Subject: Yes.

Charles: Was your father a success when his business failed?

Subject: No.

Charles: Then does having your own business guarantee success?

Subject: No.

Charles: Okay. Then can you be a success without having your own business?

Subject: Yes, but it sure helps if you have your own business.

Charles: Does having your own business guarantee success?

Subject: No.

Charles: And your father has failed in business?

Subject: Yes.

Charles: And your father said you should have your own business?

Subject: Yes.

Charles: And your father said you would be a success if you had your own business?

Subject: Yes.

Charles: How does your father know what you should do?

Subject: He doesn't.

Charles: So, how do you feel since you are unable to do what you should do?

Subject: Like a failure.

Charles: You feel like a failure?

Subject: Yes.

Charles: You feel like a failure if you don't have your own business?

Subject: Yes.

Charles: Who said you were a failure if you did not have your own business?

Subject: My father.

Charles: Your father, who failed in business, who went bankrupt in business, and then went elsewhere to set up another business, said you are a failure if you don't have your own business?

Subject: Yes.

Chatter: How would he know?

Subject: I guess he wouldn't.

Charles: And can you be a failure and still have your own business?

Subject: Yes.

Charles: So, if you had money and didn't have your own business, would you be a success?

Subject: Yes.

Charles: Is what you are really saying that you want to have more
    money?

Subject: Yes.

Charles: Do you have to have your own business to be a success?

Subject: No.

Charles: So, how do you feel about the fact you are not doing
    what you think you should be doing by having your own
    business?

Subject: Fine.

Once again, we can see the major on-going influence significant adults from childhood can have on the present and how we
view ourselves in the present. The subject felt he needed to have
his own business in order to be a success and to prove to his
father he could be a success. The subject knew his father had
failed in business, yet still felt that having his own business was
the measure of success which would gain him his father's respect.

Remember, nobody knows what we "should do."

Each of us is the one who chooses what we will do.

"If"/"When"

In terms of being counter-productive, the word, "if," serves
double duty. There are two ways in which we can use "if" to limit
our movement through life.

The first of these is the if only" game:

"If only I had done. . . ."

"If only I had known. . . ."

When we use "if" in this manner, we are back to beating up
on ourselves. We are saying whatever action we took in the past
was "not good enough." We are once again taking present
moment information and applying it to something which hap-

pened in the past. Using "if" this way denies the power of the NOW moment. What we have in this framework is a PAST, no Present, no Future.

The other not-so-functional use of "if" is when we place control of our lives outside of ourselves. It is at this point we play the "if"/"when" game:
> "When I have a new car, I'll be a success."
> "When I make another $5,000 per year, I'll be a success."
> "If I have a good relationship, I'll be happy."
> "If you love me, I'm lovable."

When we do this, we are expecting something, or someone, outside of ourselves, to provide our love, happiness, or success for us. This is not really possible. Whatever we cannot find within ourselves, we will not find outside of ourselves. The way I like to illustrate this point in the workshops is to ask: "How many of you know some one who has said something like this? When/if I make $5,000 more per year, I'll be a success." Most attendees say they do, and I continue: "Okay, now it's a year later and that person is making the additional $5,000 per year. Are they a success, or did the definition of success change?" Great laughter usually follows.

To the extent that our goals in life are external, we have given away our Personal Power. Whatever it is which we say will "make" us happy, loved, successful, or whatever else, controls our lives and has power over us.

The best story I heard regarding this point was told me by a minister: "I was 9 years old and fishing off the bank of the Ohio River with a tree branch for a pole, string for a fishing line, a cork for a bobber, and a safety pin for a hook. I was catching more fish than I could eat, and I looked up and saw a man in a rowboat with a rod and reel out in the middle of the river. I watched him fishing out there, and I thought to myself: someday, someday.

After college, I moved to Ft. Lauderdale, Florida, and sold used cars. I was very good at it, and I ended up years later with several auto dealerships of my own. I owned a nice house on the channels not far from the Intercoastal, and I had a 32-foot boat sitting at my dock. Every Friday afternoon, I took off and went deep sea fishing. One Friday, as I turned a corner in the channel, I saw a brand new 45-foot boat sitting at my neighbor's dock. As I went past it, I found myself thinking: someday, someday. It was then I realized why I had always failed to be content with my life and had never felt like I was a success."

If we get what we want, will it really provide us with what we think it will? Consider the following:

Subject: If I have more money, I will be happy.

Charles: How do you know more money will assure you happiness?

Subject: Because I just said so.

Charles: What evidence do you have that money will bring you happiness?

Subject: Because lack of money brings unhappiness.

Charles: Can you think of a time when you did not have money and you were happy?

Subject: I don't know. Maybe as a child, but I can't swear to it.

Charles: Can you think of a time as an adult when you had less money than you do now and you were happy?

Subject: I can't really say that I can.

Charles: Can you think of a time as an adult when you had more money than you do now and you were unhappy?

Subject: Yes.

Charles: Then will more money assure you happiness?

Subject: No. (pause) Oh, I see.

Do we want happiness "someday," or are we willing to accept it NOW?

"But"

The word "but" is not only counter-productive, it is also a way to counter-example ourselves. Counter-exampling is when take the power out of a compliment by what we say in response, or by adding to the compliment after the word, "but."

"I really like your dress, but don't you think it's a little busy?"

The second part of the sentence wiped out the first part. I extended a compliment, then took it back.

I can do the same thing in reverse when you compliment me.

"Charles, I really like your tie."
"This old thing?"

I did not accept your compliment. I turned it aside. I can do the same thing internally when you praise me by thinking:

"If you really knew me, you wouldn't say all these nice things."

How many times have we done this in our lives? How many times have we refused to accept compliments given us, or praise we received, because it would require us to revise the negative self-image we have of ourselves? Is this really how we want to live our lives?

"*Maybe*"

"Maybe" makes our list of counter-productive words be-cause it is a word which conveys nothing. Who can tell what "maybe" means? Not me. Therefore, "maybe" introduces us to a set of words and responses which I call DELAY RESPONSES.

A delay response is an answer which is not an answer. It is an attempt to put off answering directly whatever question has been asked or addressing whatever issue is presently being discussed. Such responses include:

"Maybe."

"I'm not ready yet."

"I don't know what you mean."

"We'll talk about it later."

"I don't know."

"I'll have to think about it."

"I don't understand."

"Whatever."

Such a response is an ineffective communication technique as it does not answer anything. It is usually an attempt to evade answering. When we receive a delay response, we might choose to ask questions to gain further information. Such questions might include:

What does "maybe" mean?

When, specifically, will "later" be?

What stops you from knowing what I mean?

"Think" about what?

What evidence do you have which tells you you are "not ready?"

How will you know when you are "ready?"

We will often find that when somebody gives us a delay response, they are saying they do not feel worthy and there is a piece of themselves within them which blocks, or prevents, a sense of being worthy. A delay response is a way to evade whatever the issue may be.

I know from my own experience that when I used to say to my former wife, "We'll talk about it later," it really meant the conversation was over and I did not want to talk about it. This, of course, left a great many issues without discussion between her and I.

There are times when a delay response can be a perfectly valid answer. For example, I usually mail out proposal packets a year before I am in an area to present workshops. Many organizations do not book speakers and presenters a year in advance, so when I call them to follow-up they tell me they are "not ready" to make a decision on that. I then ask when would be a good time to call them back, and follow up in the time frame they give to me.

When we find ourselves giving a delay response, we might choose to look within ourselves and see what we are uncomfortable with within the given situation, because we are delaying concluding the conversation or the business at hand.

No Answer

This is closely related to delay responses, and is, perhaps, the most confusing communication technique we will come across. There are people who give no answer at all. They just ignore what has been said or whatever question has been asked.

It is interesting to note many of the churches I contact regarding the workshops use this method of communication. When I am attempting to follow up on the proposal packet I sent, they do not respond at all. I may leave many messages for the decision maker with the office staff, and still never hear anything back. Some of them used to tell me they did not return my phone calls because I am seldom at home and they were not going to "waste" their money by leaving messages on my answering machine. I got an 800 number for them to call at no expense to them or their churches, and many still give no answer.

While it is true we can assume no answer means "no," it would be far more direct to simply state an answer.

I would urge each of us to remember: NO ANSWER IS NOT AN ANSWER AS IT LEAVES IN PLACE WHATEVER WAS TRANSPIRING BEFORE; WHATEVER THE QUESTION IS, IT REMAINS UNANSWERED!!!

Nuclear Words/Absolute Language

Nuclear words are the absolutes of our language. They leave no room for discussion when they are used. We might want to take a close look any time someone else uses any of the following words:

ALL,
ALWAYS,
NEVER,
EVERYBODY,
NOBODY.

To share how these words function, please consider the following discussion from a workshop.

Charles: If, for example, I say to you that everybody is doing something, and you know you are not doing it and your best friend is not doing it, you know the statement is false. I have made an absolute statement and you are not doing it already, so the statement is incorrect. I am using absolute language to try and convince you to do something I want you to do.

Subject: I frequently use "always," and it gets me in trouble with my husband. It's kind of a trigger and we end up in an argument.

Charles: Let's take a look at absolute statements. What is the structure of an absolute statement? We'll use your always, as in "It's always this way." How much room for discussion is there after this statement? It takes no prisoners once you place the word, "always," in there.

Subject: That's just the way it is.

Charles: That's the way it is. It's "always" that way.

Subject: But what if it seems like it is always that way?

Charles: Okay, what did you just say?

Subject: What if it seems like it is always that way?

Charles: Is there a difference between what you just said and saying it has just "always" been that way?

Subject: Oh, yes, because I said, "it seems."

Charles: Right, so there is a difference.

Subject: Yes.

Charles: Might the conversation be left more open if you were to say "it seems like it is always x or y" rather than making such a blanket statement? Or another way of stating a near absolute would be, "You know, most of the time, it seems like x." Now we have not thrown a nuclear weapon into the conversation. Do you see the difference?

Subject: Yes.

Charles: You're on the receiving end of it. If you use an "always," I'm going to be you, due to normal conversational patterns, after your "always," he comes back with "never." This is another absolute, so he has now lobbed his nuclear weapon also. Now the two of you can have a wonderful argument.

Subject: I don't know.

Charles: A lot of times when one person uses the word "always," they then receive back a nuclear weapon which includes the word "never."

>You always do x.

>You never do y.

Well, maybe this is true, and maybe it isn't. Both sides have thrown their nuclear weapons. Now the conversation is out of hand, and neither side is listening to the other side. Absolute statements are not productive for good communication. They are nuclear in their scope, and they take no prisoners. Further, they leave you no place to go in the conversation. You are now at the point where somebody has to be right and somebody has to be wrong, and there is no middle ground. In effective communication, when we are dealing with other people, we are trying to find the middle ground where neither person has to give up anything and we can openly and honestly discuss what we are experiencing and what we are feeling. This doesn't mean we aren't entitled to our own opinion. It just means we need to know the use of such words can lead to the end of useful conversation. People feel pre-emited, or they feel attacked. If your husband said to you, "You never do x," how would you feel?

Subject: Defensive.

Charles: If you say to him, "You always do y," how do you think he is going to feel?

Subject: Defensive.

Charles: Okay, do you see what is happening to the quality of your communications? Do you see how it is possible I call absolute statements, Nuclear?

Subject: Yes.

Charles: And do you see how you might improve the quality of your communications by not using such words?

Subject: Yes. Thank you.

"I Want"

Most people can tell me what they "don't want" far more easily than they can tell me what they "want." Most people have spent most of their lives trying to avoid certain results or consequences rather than achieving results. If I were to ask them what they wanted, most of them would then tell me what they did not want.

Most of us have noticed in our own lives how we end up achieving those things we do not want. Consider: if what we do not want is what we are focusing our attention on, guess where we are placing our energies?

I am reminded of a woman I met who did not want to be divorced. Her husband had left her three years before. He had moved in with another woman and fathered a child with that woman. Still, after the woman told me all this and I asked her what it was she wanted, she told me, "I don't want a divorce." Her feeling was that a divorce would mean she had "failed." Asked what she "wanted," she would answer:

"I don't want a divorce."

"I don't want to be a failure."

"I don't want to be alone."

This sounds pretty much like the conversation most of us are holding with ourselves most of the time. When we do so, we keep ourselves trapped. How much more could we achieve in life if we were to state what we "want," thereby creating a much more positive message to ourselves.

Even when we begin to state what we "want" in the positive, we often deny ourselves what we want by establishing a string of rationalizations (reasons) which prevent (stop) us from having those things we want. Yet, if it is something we really want, and we have all this "stuff" we are stacking on it to prevent ourselves from having it, we need to find out what it is which stops us.

Charles: What do you want?

Subject: I want a new car.

Charles: What stops you?

Subject: The payments will be too high.

Charles: So, you want a new car, and you feel the payments will be too high. If the payments weren't a problem and you felt you could afford the payments for a new car, what stops you?

Subject: I think it might be my ego that wants a new car because there is nothing wrong with my present car.

Charles: Okay, if the payments were no problem and you didn't think it was your ego which wanted the new car, what stops you from buying a new car?

Subject: Nothing.

Usually, we will find that nothing stands in our way of getting what we want unless we let it. What occurred in the example was we found out what information the subject was paying attention to which was preventing him from getting a new car. If we string an extremely long list of rationalizations/reasons together to prevent ourselves from having something, it is very likely we really do not want it. If this is so, we might choose to analyze the situation and see how it is possible we could say we want something we do not really want. Most people do not take this step, so they never find out what is stopping (preventing) them from having what they say they want. If you do not know what is stopping you, you cannot address it, move through it, and beyond it. It is only by discovering what we allow to prevent us from getting what we want that we can then have what we want.

Turning Negatives to Positives

Many times we make negative statements about ourselves. For whatever reason, we have come to believe there are things about ourselves which are undesirable. Still, depending on how we choose to view it, any negative statement we might make about ourselves can be turned into a positive resource.

Subject: I don't have enough self-confidence to speak in public.

Charles: So, you don't have enough self-confidence to speak in public? I'm really glad you shared that with me, and I want you to consider what this is telling you and what you are saying. Are you saying you have self-confidence at other times?

Subject: Yes.

Charles: So, this means you do have self-confidence as a resource under certain circumstances.

Subject: Yes.

Charles: When, specifically, do you feel self-confident?

Subject: When I'm at work and working on my computer.

Charles: You feel self-confident when you are working on the computer?

Subject: Yes.

Charles: And you don't feel self-confidence when you have to speak in front of a group of people?

Subject: Right.

Charles: What's the difference? If I put you up in front of a group of people, what will be lacking that's present when you are at work with your computer? How is it possible there is any difference? And what is the difference?

Subject: I think people will look at me and might criticize me, one way or another.

Charles: Then what you're really saying about speaking in public is you are afraid others are going to criticize you. And it doesn't really have anything to do with speaking in public, and has everything to do with being criticized.

Subject: Yes.

Charles: If you're going to be criticized, does this mean you don't want to express your opinions?

Subject: I guess I want to express my opinions. I just don't want to be criticized.

Charles: Is what you're really saying that you want to be accepted without criticism?

Subject: Yes.

Charles: So, this isn't about public speaking, and it isn't about being criticized; it's about being accepted. Does everyone always have to accept everyone else?

Subject: No.

Charles: If somebody spoke out on a matter you felt strongly about and took a point of view opposite your opinion, and, if only by speaking out would your point of view have a chance of being heard, would you speak out then?

Subject: Well, I guess so.

Charles: Then there are conditions under which you would stand up and say something in public and it won't matter what other people said.

Subject: Yes.

See, if we will explore the options we have present in our lives, we will find we have far more talents, abilities, and possibilities than we have previously allowed ourselves to realize.

Descriptive vs Interpretive Language

As we have just seen, beyond specific words, there are entire language patterns which can be counter-productive for effective communication. We can ask ourselves, are we describing what is happening, or are we interpreting it?

DESCRIPTIVE	INTERPRETIVE
arms crossed	closed off
legs crossed	embarrassed
foot movement	amused
smiling	happy
head movement	nervous
hands folded	scared

There is a big difference between these lists. While we may describe someone as having their arms crossed, thereby physically describing what is occurring, we can come up with endless variations of how we could interpret this action:

angry
closed off
bored
thinking
cold (trying to stay warm)

What is happening is we are interpreting the physical action based on our personal Belief system. We are mind-reading another person and attributing a psychological state to a physical action. We are Perceiving the actions as words, then Believing the actions to mean certain things.

We fall into the same mind set when we deal with the good/bad, right/wrong framework. The only place where each of us can define good/bad, right/wrong is within the context of our own Beliefs. When we say that something somebody else is doing means a certain thing, what we are actually saying is that if we did the same thing, the same way, under the same conditions, this is what it would mean to us. In order to find out what it means to someone else, we must ASK them what it means to them. When we fail to ask, we lose a lot of detail and may lose rapport with other people.

There is an old saying that whenever two people are together, there are six people present:

each person as they are,
each person as they see themselves,
and each person as they see t̶h̶e̶m̶s̶e̶l̶v̶e̶s̶. *the other person*

Add a few more people to the mix, and the possibilities become endless. While there may be a common definition according to Webster, language runs through the same Perceptual Filter the rest of our lives do, and we may have much less in common with each other than we think we do—unless we take the time to find out what things mean to other people.

When we go to good/bad, right/wrong language patterns, it means we have an investment in being right, in having things be a certain way. For if we have to be right, then any one who holds a view opposed to ours must be "wrong." As the other person may be doing the same thing, both sides must "dig in" in order to be "right" and make the other one "wrong." How much chance is there of communicating under these circumstances? As long as we must be right, and others must be wrong, all communication will be strained.

I prefer to look at communication as being productive/counter-productive, appropriate/inappropriate for what is occurring. I look at my personal actions the same way. If I can extend this to other people, realizing that they, too, are viewing their view of the world as productive and appropriate, then any conversation between us has a much better chance of being mutually satisfying.

3

Love
and the Possible You

*L*OVE. The word strikes fear in many of our hearts. One of the primary ways we externalize ourselves is when we are romantically involved. The other person becomes out definition of Love, of Self, and we feel "lost" without them. The other person becomes our "grape jelly." Yet, it is not so.

It is not possible to Love somebody else more than we Love ourselves. The Love we have to give is a reflection of our ability to Love ourselves, to Trust ourselves. The Love we have to give is the outer direction of our inner state of being.

Basically, Love is a matter of ACCEPTING rather than EXPECTING. Expectations are traps which we build for ourselves and for others. When we first meet, and are attracted to, another person, we "accept" them for who, and what they are. As time passes, we start to "expect" them to change certain behaviors, or change in certain ways, to please us, to "prove" they Love us. Once we start to "expect'" things of other people, we have placed conditions both on the Love we can give and the Love we can receive. We impose these limits within the framework of our Self-Trust. The more we Trust ourselves, the less we will find we "expect" of others.

Often, we "expect" some other person to "always be there" for us. We want this person to be forever close to us, and we try to hold on to him/her. When this occurs, we are showing our lack of security in the relationship. We are also showing a total lack of appreciation for the unique nature of that person.

Consider, if a butterfly lands in my hand, and I leave my hand open, I can appreciate the beauty of the butterfly. I "accept" the butterfly's state of being and the fact it might fly off again. If, however, I close my hands around it, "expecting" to hold it forever, it franticly beats its wings attempting to escape. As I open my hands, the butterfly falls to the ground, its wings destroyed by its beating them against the inside of my hands. It is no longer a thing of beauty. I would have killed the very object I sought to possess, destroying the great beauty which honored me with its presence.

If we have no desire to possess, we can have no fear of loss. The more possessive a relationship, the more fear there is of loss. Both the possessive nature of a relationship, and the fear of loss, can usually be traced to the point when we moved from "accepting" another person to "expecting" them to change for us.

Mixed Signals

Nobody can know us better than we know ourselves. What can happen is we choose to ignore certain parts of ourselves. We choose to ignore certain information, while other people are paying attention to that same information.

Perhaps we have a friend, and the observable Behavior says the friend has become romantically interested in us. We ask the friend about it, and the friend says, "Oh no, I'm not interested." Then the friend continues the Behavior. What is happening? What are we paying attention to? Do we listen to what is said, or do we respond to the actions. This is incongruent Behavior, and when things are incongruent, people can send out mixed messages.

Mixed messages can be a real problem because they work at a subconscious level and then, at the conscious level, as we are saying, "No, this is not the person I want." Yet, maybe we are flirting, or maybe they really are what we want, but we are busy saying, "No, no, this isn't what I want. This isn't my dream mate who is physically perfect and looks just the way I want." And we then say, "No, I'm not interested."

In truth, we are.

Thus, we are sending out mixed messages and other people are paying attention to the non-verbal information.

Now, if we are involved with such a person, we do so at our own risk, because if they choose to continue to ignore what they are really feeling and the signals they are sending us as a result of that feeling, they are not going to respond to us.

Recognize if we choose to accept these signals and we recognize them for what they are, we also have the responsibility to understand the other person may not even accept they are sending out such signals. They may not be capable of handling the relationship they are saying they want, or do not want, or both. And that is their problem. Our problem is coping with the mixed signals.

When we are coping with mixed signals, we may end up "mind reading" another person, or indirectly asking them to read our mind. We are not doing ourselves, or anybody else, any favors when we "mind read" them for we are attributing something to another person without having any real basis for it. To avoid this, we need to be as specific as possible with what we say to other people, and we need to ask other people questions which will allow us to know what they are really saying to us. We need to express our emotions, to say what we feel. Most people cannot say, "I Love you." What is wrong with these words? We cannot say it, but we will imply it because if we do not "say" it, we do not have to "own" it. If we do not tell somebody something directly, if we deny it as a part of ourselves, we can deny we ever felt anything. Thus, we imply, they imply, and everybody is left "mind reading" what the other person is trying to express.

In our relationships, "mind reading" can be taken a step further. Most men are brought up to be "logical." They are told, "Be a man." And, being a man, means they are not supposed to show their emotions because to do so is not macho. Boys are taught in order to be a man they are not to show, or express, emotions. In short, men are taught to "stuff" any emotions they might have.

Women, on the other hand, are told, and taught, "Be coy, be aloof, be feminine." Again, the message is to never let anybody else know what is being felt. Women hear, "Don't come out and say what you mean to men, dear. Keep men guessing." Or, as several of my students have put it, "You gotta know how to play the game," and the name of the game is "Keep the Man Guessing," never let him know what you feel. Too often, women are told they will get hurt, or men will treat them badly, if they tell men how they feel. Thus, they do not say anything, and they do not get hurt.

So, what happens? Here are all the men who do not know how to express themselves, and here are all the women who want to hear somebody express themselves, but are not willing to express themselves either. So, what happens? Nobody expresses anything!!!

The end result of these two representational systems working against each other is nobody expresses anything they really feel. Everybody ends up mind reading everybody else. Nobody has the right to say, "Gosh, I Love you," because it is too big a risk, and when people take that risk, they are likely to end up being very vulnerable.

We learned this. We learned we are vulnerable the minute we say anything, the minute we are willing to express Love to another person. What is the alternative? Shut down? Not feel?

That is what we are looking at. This is what is out there if we refuse to express what we feel and allow everything to become a matter of "mind reading." All of this occurring just because we send out mixed signals.

The Differences Between
Men & Women

This is not a matter of Mars and Venus. This list is based on the conversations I have had with thousands of people all across the United States. I would contend there are three major differences between men and women.

1) Men "think." (logic)
   Women "feel." (intuition)

Most men are almost totally uncomfortable with what they "feel." They would much rather "think" than "feel." The reason for this will be discussed fully in the next chapter. In doing so, they cut themselves off from a major portion of themselves and the information they would receive.

When I say women "feel," I am not saying they do not also "think." They are more open to both options, and far more likely to receive information from their "feelings." And they are far more likely to act on such information.

pander much, Chuck?

2) When a relationship ends, men tend to feel rejected, and women tend to feel abandoned. This seems to reflect the previous difference because "rejection" seems to be more of an intellectual process than "abandonment." "Rejection" as a mental process is more quickly worked through and can be turned into something being wrong with the other person so there is no reason to look at what we we're doing.

3) Men define themselves by their work, while women define themselves by their family and their relationships. As a general rule, women will put their loved ones above anything else in their lives. First, this will mean their boyfriend or husband. Later, this will include their children. Women are much more likely to structure their lives around their family, even if they work.

Men, on the other hand, usually make their primary definition of themselves their employment. This most likely stems from the age-old concept of the man being the provider for the family. Men's self-worth usually can be far more damaged by their employment than by their relationship.

And, ladies, usually the best to be hoped for is second place behind the job; however, if there is some sort of athletic interest, you may be coming in third.

While no list is absolute, I think we can see how conflict could arise in our Love relationships out of such differences.

Power Positions

Power, Power, who has the Power?

If we want to know who has the Power in a relationship, we can often tell by looking at how people hold themselves physically in relationship to each other. And even as I say this, I would again remind the reader that body language is not an absolute. It is, however, a guideline.

I contend Powerfulness and Powerlessness are both learned Behaviors and most of us got a very powerful message regarding Power and who has it. As children, we all received a gender neutral message regarding Power. We were small, and we lived in a land run by giants. The giants (adults) made the rules. The giants enforced the rules. As far as we knew, the giants might be God, for they certainly controlled what happened in our world. In short, as a child, we learned that size was Power.

All of us, male and female, received this impression when we were children. Now we have grown up and become the adults, the big people, the giants, and we are still carrying this message with us. As men are normally physically larger than women, and most of us Believe size is Power due to the indirect message received as children, most women feel a degree of Powerlessness in their relationships with men.

It is not true.

It is only a Perception.

And it still affects us.

I have met men who normally are very kind and considerate, yet when they get into a primary relationship they become controlling and manipulative.

I once counselled a female Air Force pilot: "Charles, I'm a strong and competent woman. The United States Government entrusts me with multi-million dollar equipment. Yet, when I get into a male-female relationship, I feel like a complete and total dummy."

The message is that strong, and we carry it with us. It can get in the way of our having a mutually satisfying co-equal relationship.

And, here is a method we can use to assist ourselves in gaining a new and more Powerful Perception: stand on a chair. Really, stand on a chair, thus making us "bigger" than those about us. Doing this will make most people feel far more "Powerful." Once we realize this, we can begin to make Powerfulness a permanent resource in our lives.

Ladies, to "equalize" a serious discussion, make sure both of you are sitting down, or, better still, stand on a step to "equalize" size. Women doing this will often see the man become uncomfortable in cases like this because he feels a loss of "Power," and, thus, of control.

Still, the Fact remains, in a truly "equal" relationship, we don't need to control our partner, and we do not need Power over other people. We find our sense of Self within and then share it with others.

"what's Important"

What is important to us in a relationship? What are we looking for in another person? What has to "be there" for us to want to enter a long-term committed relationship?

Tough questions, and they are questions many of us are asking ourselves as we date, as we interact socially. When I ask these questions in a workshop, we usually end up making a list of what we believe is important.

    caring
    open
    honest
    trustworthy
    loving
    sense of humor
    communicative
    spiritual
    truthful
    fidelity

After the list is on the board, and everyone is pretty much agreeing these are "what's important" in a relationship, I pick one person to talk with, and the conversation usually goes like this:

Charles: This state has a lottery, doesn't it?
Subject: Yes.
Charter: Do you ever buy a lottery ticket?
Subject: Only when it's a very large pot.
Charles: Okay, great. Let's say there's a lottery jackpot of $40,000,000.00, and you have the only winning ticket. You're going to get $2,000,000.00 per year for the next 20

years. After taxes, you'll have about $1,000,000.00 a year. Do you think you can manage to scrape by on that?

Subject: (laughing) Oh, yeah, I sure think so.

Charles: Well, there is this car you have always wanted to get. You know the car I'm talking about. It's a really HOT car!! Do you know the car I am talking about?

Subject: Oh, yes.

Charles: And this is a really HOT car. You go down to the auto dealership with the cash in your pocket to buy this car. You approach the salesperson and begin to describe the car: AM-FM radio, 6-disk CD player, dual cassette with auto reverse, the best stereo speakers available, leather interior, power windows, power seats with 10-position adjustment, a performance package with every extra there is, and the car goes from 0 to 60 in 2.2 seconds. Is this the car you want?

Subject: Yeah, that's it.

Charles: The salesperson is getting very excited as you describe this car because he has just the car out on the lot. The car is almost a one of a kind, really expensive, the commission on it is more than he usually makes in a month. The car you want is right out there on the lot. Are you excited?

Subject: You bet.

Charles: And you get out to the car and the car is grey. Do you buy the car?

Subject: No, I wanted red.

Charles: Right. Then red is what's important to you and all the features you described were simply window dressing. If you don't buy the car because it is grey, even though it had all the features, then the color is what is important!!

Most of us are doing the same type of thing in our social lives. We put up a good list of what we want in another person, and then sort differently when we get out into the world. Go back and look at the list we made earlier. These items are personality

qualities, inner qualities the person would have in their personality. Yet, when most of us are meeting people, we move over to
what I call the B list:

eye color
hair color
weight
body build
how they dress
cute
where they live
income

This second list has almost nothing to do with the first list.
The first list was based on INNER QUALITIES; the second list deals
with OUTER APPEARANCES. If the second list is what we are paying
attention to and how we are really sorting out the people we
meet, it is very hard to find a person with the qualities of the first
list. Whatever reason we have for ending a relationship, or for
not even approaching another person, is "what's important" in a
relationship to us, and all the rest is merely window dressing.

As one woman noted: "Last Friday, my husband and I went
out to a club with some friends. It's the first time in several years
we've gone out because we're so busy taking care of the kids.
Anyway, I was walking around and I hardly knew anybody, right?
Just to have fun, just to try and be myself. I mean, they didn't
know who I was. They had no idea that I'm married as I'm going
around. They can't tell if I'm with someone or not because I'm
with a group of people. So, if I tried to talk with someone, just
talk, not even like some sort of come-on, there's this wall; and,
it's like, unless I'm interested in you, or think I'd be interested in
you, sexually, I can't respond. It was just so weird to feel that; and
people, when they could just be having fun and making friends,
all they wanted was sex, or to look good, to be seen with the right
people. It was rather sad and sort of depressed me. You could

meet these same people under other circumstances, and it would be so different. I was kind of shocked by the shallowness of it all."

And there was a man who came for counselling. He very much wanted to have a good relationship, yet every time he got into one, it would end. He was very depressed. He could not understand what was preventing him from having a fulfilling primary relationship.

I asked him what was important in a relationship to him. He went into great detail, giving me many items from both lists. As I continued to write, I became confused because I also knew the last two women he had dated and both of them met both the Inner Qualities and the Outer Appearances he was describing for me. Confused, I pointed this out to him and asked him what the reason was that he had broken up with either of them.

He explained: "Well, neither one of them can have any children. They've both had their tubes tied. And I want to have children, so I broke off with each of them."

In his case, the biological ability of a woman to bear him a child was what was important because it was the reason he would leave an otherwise suitable relationship.

WHAT'S IMPORTANT to you?

"Distance"

One of the reasons many of us turn away from otherwise productive and fulfilling relationships is the matter of "distance." We seem to feel that if there is a physical distance between us and the one we love, somehow this will make the relationship less than what we want.

A man shared this experience: "I travel doing workshops for a living. Several years ago, I met a woman who attended a workshop I did in St. Louis. She asked for my address. I gave it to her, and she actually wrote me. I wrote back, and that began an on-going correspondence between us. At first, we wrote each other about every four to six weeks, then it was every three or four weeks, and by the time I was going to St. Louis to do another workshop two years later, we were writing about every ten days. I was there for just a few days, and the relationship grew closer. I rent a fishing cabin near Mountain Home, Arkansas, for part of every summer and invited her to join me for a week. She accepted, but then could not come when it turned out she had to have an operation for cervical cancer. I broke off my fishing, and went up to St. Louis to be there for her during her recovery. I stayed with some friends of mine and saw her every afternoon and/or evening for a week. It was wonderful. It was the supportive, loving relationship, and we begin to talk about my moving to St. Louis and the possibility of a life together.

"It was two days before I was to leave. We had been out to dinner and were sitting on a park bench overlooking the Mississippi River. All of a sudden, she turned to me and said, 'I can't do this.'

"I stopped, looked at her, and asked, 'Can't do what?'

"She then explained to me that she could not do a long-distance relationship, that I was leaving and was not going to 'be there' for her.

"I was shocked. I was floored. And I knew there was nothing I could do about it. I talked to her, but her mind was already made up. All of a sudden, all that mattered about our relationship was my physical location."

What happened to him, happens to many of us, for most people will trade their Passion for physical presence. While physical presence does not assure emotional, spiritual, psychic, or intellectual closeness or supportiveness, we often trade all the others just to have somebody who will "be there."

We pay a high price for this. Many of us "spend" our lives in relationships which "share" little or nothing.

Do we want Quantity or Quality in our relationships?

Loving/"In Love"

Most of the people I know who are "in Love" do very unloving things to each other on a regular basis. It seems that when we are "in Love" with another person, they become an object. They are the "object" of our Love. They are no longer a person, rather an object, a treasure to be placed in a museum, thus freezing the moment in time. If the person changes in any manner, they are no longer the person we "fell in Love with." Now dare they change. Now dare they stop being the person I met, or thought I met.

"Loving," on the other hand, is a state of Beingness and acceptance, both of the other person and ourselves. "Loving" exists in the NOW moment and accepts Change and Growth in the other person as a part of the natural evolution of the relationship.

How "Loving" are we willing to be?

Flirting/Secondary Gains:
A Conversation

Charles: Going back to last week, we were talking about flirting. You said you are a tremendous flirt and the secondary gain to flirting is attention. Right?

Subject: Yes.

Charles: If we can find a way to assist you in seeing there are other ways of getting attention, or that flirting may be counter-productive behavior, then we can assist you in finding other ways to gain attention in a more positive manner without a potentially self-destructive behavior.

Subject: I think I understand.

Charles: Well, I understand, and this was something which was mentioned last week, which is the only reason I use it as an example now. I used you because we started talking about this last week and you said you used to be a tremendous flirt. It does not mean you have to be a flirt now. This is a past pattern, and you have already broken it. Still, let's look at the structure of the experience. With anybody who is a tremendous flirt, the underlying secondary gain is usually getting attention.

>   Flitting   (specific Behavior)
>   Attention   (secondary gain)

Flirting. The secondary gain to flirting is attention. If we can find a way into the representational system to match the secondary gain, the Attention the person is getting, and also show them how flirting may actually be counter-productive for what they really want. So, we have two things going on. One, the specific Behavior, which is flirting. Two, the secondary gain, which is to get Attention. How is it possible the person wants to get Attention? There is a secondary gain to getting Attention

Subject: That's what I was thinking. You need to find out why the person was flirting and craving attention.

Charles: Right. They crave attention. Most people who flirt are really seeking attention. Yet, in most cases, if you really get down in the Representational System, they want Love. They want to feel Loved. And, so, because they want to feel Loved, they flirt to get attention, and that attention, to them, constitutes Love.

>   Flirting   (specific. Behavior)
>   Attention   (secondary gain)
>   Love   (underlying issue)

Now, the question would be are they getting the Love they need by flirting? The answer is no, probably not. What they are going to get is a lot of superficial attention. They are going to attract, male or female, other people who are superficial, and they are not going to find Love or any type of permanent relationship. See, in desiring Love and wanting attention, what is the true core issue? What is it these people are really looking for? Security.

Flitting   (specific Behavior)
Attention   (secondary gain)
Love   (underlying issue)
Security   (core issue)

Most of us have this piece in place. I'm not saying this is bad, because we are back to where there isn't really any good or bad. This is just a state of Beingness as we look for a Secure interpersonal relationship. And there can be a lot of give and take in this.

Friend: And it can also become a vicious circle because the flirting gives them attention, and out of that attention, they get superficial Love. Then, when it's over, they feel even worse because the attention is gone and they once again feel the lack of Love, and they feel the need to flirt again to gain attention.

Subject: Wow, yes, That's exactly the way it was.

Charles: Yes, and we all know people who are stuck in the cycle, repeating it endlessly.

Flirting

Attention

And until they break that cycle, they're stuck!! Consider how very lonely that can be. (to subject) Did you ever really feel fulfilled when you were in that cycle?

Subject: Nothing lasting. There was always something missing. I mean, it was superficial. I mean, it was wonderful to flirt and to have a conquest from the flirting by getting attention. That was fulfilling in itself, but then when I went home, that's it, I was still alone. I never got enough to where I felt there was enough. I was always looking for Love and Security. Now, I no longer have the need to go out and be a flirt. If I see flirting coming back into my Behavior, I know I need to look at how Secure I'm feeling and what I'm paying attention to which allows me to feel that way.

Control And Loneliness: A Discussion

Charles: There are two key issues which you keep mentioning: Control and Loneliness. Loneliness. How do we end up with Loneliness? When we are in any type of relationship, we have two people interacting with each other.

These circles represent the sum total of each person's personality. Where the circles touch is where we interact with another person. Where we touch people, we have a common interest, and that is the part of ourselves we choose to share. And, in order for every aspect of our lives to be touched, for every interest we have to be addressed, it means we may need to interact with a number of different people. No matter how good our relationship is with any one person, they are not going to meet every need we have. If we think they will, we are not being realistic.

Now, this state of separation between something on the far side of the other persons circle and something on the far side of ours, that is Loneliness. It is that feeling of separation. We can be with somebody we are very close to and still feel lonely, because no matter how close we are, there is still that space. People get married hoping that will end the loneliness. The circles still represent us and another person, and while there may be a bigger overlap of interest in marriage than there is in just a friendship, there are still those isolated places on the opposite ends. We overlap. Yet, on each extreme, there are places, no matter how close we are to each other, where we feel lonely even when we are with each other because there are wants and needs and desires and interests which are not really being addressed. This is the reason it is a really good idea for a poker night, or for a girls' night out every now and then, so those things we are interested in which the significant other is not interested in can still be fulfilled. This does not mean we do not care; it just means there are places we do not share. This can be very lonely. And, many times, we do not recognize this dynamic, or we deny those feelings of loneliness because we think a given person is supposed to be everything for us.

Actually, everything any of us needs is on the inside of our own circle, inside of ourselves. We do not really *need* anybody else. We may *desire* their presence, we may like their presence, we may want to share life with them, we may feel good when they are around; yet, to "need" somebody is to place Expectations on them. To "need" them is to say, "I'm not complete without you." And that is not necessarily so. The minute we are not complete without somebody else, we just gave them our Personal Power. Sharing is a lot better than "I'll lead, you follow," so get two steps behind me and stay there. And it makes no difference which one does it.

Personal Power ties into Loneliness, because we start to get desperate as we feel lonely, and we then start to give away our Personal Power. We fall into a dynamic of "If I do X, he (she) will Love me and/or be there for me." Maybe they will. Maybe they won't. Or maybe they will be there this time, and the next time we are going to have to do something more in order for them to be there for us. Thus, we start to progressively give away our Personal Power.

Subj. 1: Perhaps one of the reasons people are drawn to this type of workshop is that people recognize the need to be able to communicate with each other better. We know there is a need, so we come to develop our skills further.

Charles: Very possible. And at the same time, the core issue we are talking about—being able to communicate, and we talk about finding the core issues, the underlying Belief, and if we have a Belief we are going to be lonely, where is it coming from? In most cases, it comes from a dynamic where we begin to reach a point where we want somebody else to be everything for us. The minute we do this, we have done a terrible thing both to ourselves and the other person. At this point, we have made certain the other person will fail us because at some point they cannot live up to everything we want. They cannot live up to our Expectations, so they must fail. When this happens, we can go back to being "not good enough," being abandoned and rejected, and having general feelings of unworthiness. See how wonderfully we can play this game, come from our past scripts, if we choose to? When we start to Expect things from another person, we have built a Trap for them, and for ourselves, and we have assured ourselves there will be Limitations in our relationships.

Subj. 2: I was just thinking when you put it that way, and I think about my own relationship, I think it makes me look like the bad guy.

Charles: How is it possible you are the bad guy?

Subj. 2: By what you just said. I mean, I really belong in this workshop.

Charles: Oh, so you said you are the bad guy. Is it, perhaps, the case that you have been expecting things from other people? Is this what I'm hearing from you? Is this what you are feeling?

Subj. 2: Yes.

Charles: Another word for Expectations is Trap. The minute we Expect something of somebody, we have stopped Accepting them for who and what they are. This happens because most of us derive our sense of Lovableness on the Love and approval we receive from outside of our sense of Self.

Is the Love we receive from others more important to us than Loving ourselves? Are we willing to allow our sense of Self to be violated, are we willing to allow ourselves to stay in non-productive relationships, in order to have "Love?"

Many of us attach our sense of Lovableness and Self-worth to the relationship we are presently in. We find ways to convince ourselves that without the "love" we have in that relationship, we will have no "love" at all. We have made another person into the only available source of Love. Is that true?

Subj. 3: Gosh, no.

Charles: When we do this, we cling to the relationship we presently have, regardless of how painful it might be, regardless of how much the other person may be abusive of us, and take advantage of us, because regardless of how uncomfortable we are in the present relationship, it is better than not having a relationship and being alone. Is it "love" when we allow ourselves to stay in an abusive relationship because we fear we can't do any better? This sense of lack becomes our "comfort zone." If we make changes, we must step out of this and into the unknown.

True Love comes from within, not from without, or from some other person. When we realize this, we can release the expectations we have of other people. Do you see what I'm saying? And I'm not casting stones. God knows, I have been there and done that.

Subj. 2: 1 understand what you're saying, but I still feel guilty in my relationship.

Charles: Is the guilt you feel productive?

Subj. 2: No.

Charles: Then what is that guilt telling you? Guilt is a way of telling ourselves when we have violated our own standards and/or Beliefs, or that somebody else has. What we can choose to look at, what might be useful for you to look at is how, specifically, when, specifically, and where, specifically, you are feeling guilty. Under what conditions are you feeling guilty? What is the trigger point? Then ask yourself: "Is this the result of an Expectation? How am I violating my own personal standards and ethics, and how am I allowing them to be violated?" You will then find out how it is possible you are feeling guilty.

One of the problems is we "should" on ourselves *all the time!* If we listen to our Self-talk, a lot of it is "shoulds." Shoulds are a form of expectations, expectations of ourselves. Often, when we are in Self-talk, what is really happening is we have gotten into our Parts of Self, and they are busy talking with each other. And one part says, "I think I'd like to do X." And another part responds, "Jeez, we already tried that once, and it didn't work." And then still another part jumps in and says, "Yeah, we tried it at 19, and it didn't work then either. There are two of us parts down here looking at this thing and we don't like it, and if you do it, you are gonna get crushed."

This is what is happening in our Experiential Framework, our past parts of Self are talking to us. This is where we are getting the feedback from. This is how it is possible it is important to go back and let the parts of Self know how things do not have to be the same in the Present as they were in the Past, or how they can be different in the Future than they are in the Present or were in the Past. As long as the Parts don't believe us, there isn't going to be any change. As long as we focus on how alone we have been in the Past, we will feel the same way in the Present.

Subj. 2: We all know what you're saying, but when we get lonely, it's hard to remember.

Charles: Well, loneliness can also be a signal to us that there might be something we want to take hold of and change in our lives. It could be as simple as recognizing that "loneliness" is a state of neediness in which we are telling ourselves we "need" the presence of another person to be whole. This "loneliness" is far different than "aloneness" which is a state of solitude. Once again, it is a function of the words we are using on ourselves, and any negative we have, we can turn into a positive, if we allow ourselves to do so.

Triggered by "Love"

A "special person" is someone who triggers (touches off) certain key sub-modalities within us. If we can find the Structure of this, we can than find out what triggers us into the feeling we "Love" another person.

While there are countless variations, there are three primary systems through which we are triggered into the "Love" state.

VISUAL EXTERNAL: This person would have to "see" it. They would have to be "shown" they are loved. Examples of such a trigger could include:
the physical appearance of the other person
being taken certain places,
being given certain things,
seeing certain physical comforts.

AUDIO EXTERNAL: This person would have to "hear" they are loved. Examples of such a trigger could include:
being told in a certain way,
hearing certain words,
hearing a certain voice tone.

KINESTHETIC EXTERNAL: This person would have to "feel" they are loved. Examples of such triggers could include:
having their hand held,
being touched a certain way,
being held a certain way,
having a certain body sensation,
being kissed a certain way.

Perhaps this does not sound very romantic; however, for us to change the direction of our relationships and our lives, we may choose to look at such triggers. To get to a "state of love" only one of the specific representational systems needs to be triggered/stimulated/set off. For those who do not believe such things are true, I would refer them to John Derek. His three wives were all the same physical type. Anyone who has ever looked at Andress, Evans, and Bo can see a very strong physical similarity.

Once we find out what it is which triggers the "love" state in ourselves, or another person, we can make ourself, or that other person, "feel loved" each and every time.

4

Feelings and the Possible You

*L*OVE IS A SPECIFIC FEELING. It is one of many feelings we can have, and the problem with feelings is that we have to "feel" them. Most of us do not want to do that. In fact, most of us do not feel that Life works or that we have the right to live our lives in a personally fulfilling and meaningful manner to ourselves as individuals. The key word here is the word "feel." I did not say we do not "think" that Life works; I said we do not "feel" that Life works.

I believe there are three levels of Knowledge. The first level is thinking, or intellect. It is head stuff. Many of the people who attend workshops believe that if they change their thinking they can change their lives. The problem with this is that as we read the books, listen to the tapes, attend the workshops, and listen to speakers, and we find something we think will work great, something we think will change our lives. And as we accept this new information on an intellectual level and move towards the change, we hear this little voice from way down deep inside: "This will never work. Nope, no way this is ever going to happen."

We have just moved into the second level of Knowledge, our feelings. And what we think and what we feel very seldom agree with each other. Thus, most of us, for most of our lives, have what I call a CIVIL WAR going on between what we think and what we feel. And as long as this war continues, we usually get mixed results when we move towards change.

What we might want to consider is that we want to get to the third level of Knowledge, which I call KNOWING. This is when what we think (intellect) and what we feel (emotion) get together and talk with each other and work together. This is a desired state; however, few of us ever get there because we are in such denial of what we feel. After all, we do not want to have any bad feelings.

I contend there is no such thing as a good feeling or a bad feeling, a right feeling or a wrong feeling. They are all just Feelings, states of Beingness, and they are all appropriate.

I made this statement on talk radio, WCKY, in Cincinnati, Ohio, some years ago. I was doing two workshops on a Thursday at St. Francis Center for Peace and Renewal, and they got me on WCKY ("All talk, all day, for Cincinnati") Wednesday afternoon, 4:00 PM to 5:00 PM, prime time, drive time, as a way to promote the workshops. I had been talking for almost 40 minutes, which is actually 25 minutes in talk radio time because talk radio has so many commercials, and absolutely nobody had called in. The hostess was surprised because Cincinnati is a fairly conservative town and what I had been saying was hardly conservative, and definitely not in keeping with "mainline" theories of change and growth. As we went to commercial, I made this statement about Feelings, ending with "and all Feelings are appropriate."

Six telephone lines lit up. We had found Cincinnati's hot button. We were going to talk about Feelings.

After the commercial, we went to caller number one, calling us from his car phone: "Charles, did you just say that all Feelings are appropriate?"

"Yes sir, I certainty did say that."

"Well, Charles, what if I get angry and I kill somebody?"

"Sir, that's two transactions. The first is the Feeling; the second is what you do with it."

Sadly, most of us have been sold the bill of goods that to feel the Feeling is to take the Action. Most of us attempt to repress our Feelings because we feel the expression of the Feeling would be wrong.

Jimmy Carter almost lost the Presidential election in 1976 because he was quoted in *Playboy* as saying, "I have lusted in my heart." People did not understand the remark, and he dropped a quick 10 points in the polls. What people overlooked was what he said after that statement: "Just because I lust in my heart when I see a beautiful woman doesn't mean I have to act on it. It does mean I have to acknowledge it so I can move beyond it."

This is very true. We cannot move beyond our Feelings until we acknowledge them. Of course, most of us are almost totally out of touch with our Feelings. I mean, we remember the last Feeling we had, what was it, 2 or 3 years ago, and it hurt, so we decided not to have another one.

Additionally, each of us were given a specific "don't feel" message as we were growing up.

Men, our "don't feel" message went something like this: "Be tough. Be strong. Be a man. Don't cry." And if we did cry: "Don't be a sissy. Don't be a girl." Thus, we got the message that to Feel a certain way was wrong or bad, and that we were weak if we had that Feeling. Ladies, please take note of this because it explains how it is possible so many men are emotionally unavailable. Once they learned how not to Feel, they also learned how to distance themselves from other people.

Women also got a "don't feel" message as they were growing up. The message went something like this: "Don't you talk back to me, young lady. Don't you raise your voice with me. Don't you get angry with me, young woman." Thus, women also learned a certain type of Feeling, certain emotions, were bad.

And once we had permission to get out of touch with one Feeling, we had permission to get out of touch with them all. We go into Denial—and Denial is not a river in Egypt.

Again, I contend all Feelings are appropriate.

Still, even if we believe this, many of us are not able to get in touch with our Feelings.

Talking with our Feelings

I want to assist in the process of learning how to make friends with our feelings. This visualization, and the ones which follow, might work best if they are tape recorded for future use.

I want you to close your eyes and go inside to that quiet place, that private place, within. And, as you go within, breathing at your own, natural breathing rate, I want you to breathe in all the Possibilities you can Be. And, as you exhale, at your own natural breathing rate, please let go of doubt, and fear, and limitation. So that every time you breathe, you are breathing in possibility and exhaling limitation.

Now, as you go within the moment, within the possibility, within the moment, please create in your mind's eye what would be, to you, a comfortable room. And please step into that comfortable room.

So, you are in a comfortable room, and please place in this room two comfortable chairs. These are chairs which would be comfortable to you as an individual. And please place these chairs close to each other and at a 60 to 90 degree angle to each other. This is considered conversational mode.

Wow! You're here in a comfortable room with two comfortable chairs, and you sit down in one of the chairs, and, boy, you sure do feel comfortable.

Now entering the room and sitting down in the other chair is your Feeling of Anger. Your Feeling of Anger has just entered the room and sat down in the other chair. Please turn to your Anger and ask it:

1) What is your functional value?

2) What do you want to teach me?

3) What do I want to learn from you?

And please listen to what your Anger tells you.

(1-minute pause)

Now, come back to the present moment, to this time and this space, bringing with you the information you have received.

What we want to remember is that every Feeling is functional, and by talking to our Feelings, by listening to the messages it has for us, we may move through it and past it into whatever comes next. As long as we refuse to acknowledge the existence of our Feelings, we will remain in a "Stuck" state.

Because Anger is an almost universally accepted negative emotion to adults, this is the reason I used it. In the workshops, many people report they cannot get their Anger to talk with them. Some report Anger just sticking its head around the corner and refusing to come in; others say it comes part way across the room, nods its head no, and turns around and walks out; and still others report is sits down and just refuses to say anything. One person told me their Anger came in as a teenager, dressed in red, and sat upside down with its head in the seat, and did not say anything. Still, this may be the closest they have been to their Anger in years. These are the people who say "I shouldn't Feel this way" when they "feel" Anger.

There is a reason for each question.

"What is your functional value?"

Every Feeling has a functional value. It carries a specific message for us. In my case, my Anger's functional value is to let me know when I feel like my sense of personal safety, or my sense of personal ethics, has been violated either by someone else, or myself. Knowing this, I can act the information. Anger is a reaction to safety and ethics issues.

I drive everywhere I go, logging 45,000 to 60,000 miles a year. There are times when suddenly somebody decides to cut across 4 or 5 lanes of traffic to exit and almost takes off the front end of my car. I am Angry. I do not have to honk my horn, flash my lights, wave my fist, give them the finger, or chase them for miles to let them know how poorly I think they drive. I do choose to admit my Anger, and then move through it and past it.

"What do you want to teach me?"

Every time we feel a Feeling it is there to teach us something. This question allows us to find out what, specifically, the feeling is there to teach us at this time. What the Feeling is there to teach can change every time we have a Feeling.

"What do I want to learn from you?"

This is a check off questions because it allows us to find out if we want to learn something the Feeling is not there to teach. When this is so, we have a conflict between what it is there to teach and what we want to learn, and we can choose to have a dialogue over this difference.

Until we can learn how to "talk" with our Feelings and accept them as a part of our functional whole, it will be almost impossible for us to move through, and beyond, them and into whatever comes next. It is only in admitting the Feeling is there that we can do anything about it. As long as we deny a Feeling, we are trapped, because in order to deny it, we must continually engage it and keep it away.

Once we admit our Feelings, once we begin to "talk" with them, we can then begin to make friends with them. Once we make friends with them, we can then invite them all in and throw a big party. Then, we can create a comfortable room with three chairs in it and invite our Head, representing our Thinking, and our Heart, representing our Feelings, and sit them down so we can get to Knowing.

Releasing a Feeling

After we have learned to "talk" with our Feelings, we may find it useful to embrace it, move through it, and then release it. Too many of us feel "trapped" by our Feelings, and have no way to "get away" from them. The following visualization is a technique for releasing a Feeling.

I want you to see yourself standing in a grassy field. Nearby, there is a hot air balloon tied to a tree by a pulley system. Actually, this hot air balloon is filled with helium. . . . You walk over next to the hot air balloon and you see a stack of boxes nearby. The boxes are marked Anger (or whatever emotion you are dealing with). . . . You start to take those boxes and load them into the basket under the balloon. Don't worry if the basket seems too small; this is a one-size-fits-all basket, and it will expand to take on as many boxes as you need to place in it. . . . Now you have loaded the boxes into the basket, and you go over to the end of the rope which is connected to the balloon and holds it in place. . . . Now, let the balloon out 10 feet, and see how you experience this. . . . And let the balloon out 100 feet, and see how you experience this. . . . And let the balloon out 100 yards, and see how you experience this. . . . Now, let go of the rope . . . let go of the rope . . . and watch as the balloon floats away . . . getting higher . . . and higher . . . and further . . . and further away . . . and the wind catches it, taking it

further away . . . and higher and further . . . higher and
further . . . it's but a dot in the distance . . .and now, it's
gone.

How do you Feel?

Funny story. One of the first times I was using this visualization, the woman I was working with responded, "It was taking
too long, so I put my stuff in a steamer trunk and kicked it over
the edge of the cliff."

I didn't know there was a cliff.

Still, it was her visualization.

Whatever works.

The Wall

One of the Feelings we seem to have the most trouble with
is a sense of connection to the rest of the world. As many of us
"shut down," we also built walls around our lives to protect
ourselves from those things which had "hurt" us. Perhaps it is
time to take those walls down.

I want you to see yourself standing behind the walls you
built around your life. . . . I want you to see those walls in all
their glory . . . because any time something got behind those
walls and hurt you, you added to those walls . . . building
them thicker and higher, thicker and higher . . . until they
were so high, and so thick, that the only time you could see
the sun was when it was directly overhead . . . so it is dark,
and kind of stinks because of all that "stuff" that was
collected. . . . Now, I've hired a bonded building crew to
take down those walls . . . and I want you to let them do that
because you know a bonded crew won't lose any of the
building materials . . . so they start to take those walls down
. . . and this can take some time because they are so thick

and so high . . . and as they come down, the materials are
piled up off to the right . . . and now the walls are down, and
you look around . . . and you discover you are on an island
. . . you are on the Island of You and surrounded by water
from the mainland . . . and in order for anybody to get here
to "hurt" you, they had to come across the water . . . so if you
had not had the walls, you might have been able to see them
coming . . . maybe we could do something else with all this
building material, so we ask the building crew to build you a
house . . . the House of your New Consciousness . . . and it
is a nice single or split-level house with lots of windows so
you can see what is coming across the water. . . . It is really
very light and airy . . . and over the front door is the word,
Love . . . and over the back door is the word, Trust . . . and
this is a really nice house . . . and you have a lot of building
material left over, and because there are times you might
want to visit the mainland, let's build a bridge . . . and
because there are times you might want to be alone, and
there are times you might feel the need for safety . . . it's a
drawbridge . . . you can take it up any time you want . . . so
you are on the Island of You with the House of your New
Consciousness, connected to the mainland by a drawbridge
. . . and you now take all that "stuff" . . . you know the
"stuff," it makes good compost . . . and you spread it out on
the bare lawn in front of the House of your New Consciousness . . . and now it is a year later and you are looking out
onto the Lawn of your Life . . . and what do you see?? . . .
What do you see??

5

The Basis of the Behavior (an example)

TO SHARE HOW ALL OF THIS COMES TOGETHER and can be used, I'd like to share an exchange which took place in a class on change and personal growth I was teaching several years ago. The names have been changed, of course, to protect the identity of those present.

Charles: So, Karen Anne, find a time in your life in which you usually respond in a way you find unsatisfactory or inappropriate. Tell me what it is. Is it something pertaining to your mother?

Karen: Yes. My mother and father, both. It's when I'm home now that I've lived away for so long. I go home, and I find myself reacting the same way I would have if I still lived there. For example, I was home at Christmas and borrowed the car to go to a movie, and I didn't mention we were going to stop and have a cocktail afterward. They got worried as it was two hours after the movie got out, and they knew it, and I wasn't home. I was feeling that fear that I should have told them when I was going out, but I didn't tell them, knowing full well they could still be awake when I got home.

Charles: What I am hearing you say is that when you go home, and you are with your parents, you find yourself acting out of old scripts where you feel you need to live up to whatever it is they are expecting of you.

Karen: I feel myself reacting the way I used to react, whether they expect it of me or not. I mean, it's just like everything: my not telling them I would be going out afterward and would be home late, and then the feeling of dread and my not enjoying it because I wasn't up front in telling them about what was going on.

Charles: When you took the car and went out and had cocktails after the movie, you were unable to enjoy yourself?

Karen: Yes.

Charles: And you had this feeling of dread?

Karen: That's a pretty exaggerated word. Not dread, just discomfort.

Charles: Okay, you had discomfort because you hadn't told them exactly what you were going to do.

Karen: Right, and I knew they would expect that since the movie was over at 9:00 PM and I would be back by 9:15 or 9:30 PM.

Charles: Okay, in that context, and in that situation, how would you like to respond?

Karen: I would like to respond either before I leave by telling them what we are planning so they don't expect us home before 11:00 PM, or I could pick up the phone, call them, and tell them what we are doing.

Charles: Which one of these options do you think would be the most productive for you?

Karen: The first one.

Charles: Okay, so telling them before you went out would be the desired state?

Karen: Yes.

Charles: Within the context of telling your parents before you go out and do something by telling them what your plans might be, what's important about doing this?

Karen: That they understand not to expect me home at a certain time and they don't have to worry when I don't arrive at the time they expect me.

Charles: Then you might say what's important would be that they have more information and there would be less worry.

.Karen: Yes, a whole lot less worry.

Charles: And if they worry less and have more information, how are they going to treat you?

Karen: More like an adult and less like when I was young and living there.

Charles: Might it be then, that what we're looking for is to be treated like an adult by our parents? Is this the desired outcome?

Karen: Yes.

Charles: The desired outcome, then, is perhaps, not the specific incident, but an overall feeling of being treated and respected as an adult. Given this, how will you know when you are being treated like an adult?

Karen: Because I won't have those awful feelings like I'm being treated like a child.

Charles: Fine. Now, how are you going to implement giving them more information?

Karen: I'll just have to reframe it the next time I'm there in that situation.

Charles: Yes.

Karen: To begin with, it's obvious if I'd said we were going out and will be back late, none of this would have ever taken place.

Charles: Hindsight's always 100% perfect. We spend far too much of our lives in 20/20 hindsight.

Marie: Can I comment?

Charles: Yes, please do.

Marie: (to Karen) Don't you think it's childish of you to take your parent's car while you're staying at their home, and you don't give them the information when you leave for the evening?

Karen: I was operating out of my 17-year-old.

Marie: See, you were acting like a child so you were expecting to be treated like a child. An adult wouldn't take somebody else's car and not tell them where they will be.

Karen: So, I'm concerned about not being treated like a child, but my actions were those of a child.

Charles: Correct. Now, you've got it.

Karen: And I was in my 17-year-old again, stuck at home, and having all of the same old feelings of what it was like before I moved away.

Charles: You gave them that power?

Karen: Yes.

Charles: Then the way to take it back would be to tell them before you go out what your plans are. And tell them as an adult, not as a child. Would that work? Can you see yourself doing that?

Karen: Sure, because they come and visit us every year, and I enjoy their visits. It gets on my nerves towards the end of the visit, but (speaks directly to Marie) you were there. This is the same type of mother-daughter relationship. I'm having a party. Craig and I live together. We invited his parents over, some personal friends including Marie and Tom, and my parents. The party lasted through the afternoon into the evening, and Mom wanted me to be up and cleaning. We still had guests and were still conversing. We were more laid back and said, "No, we'll do it later after the people leave." But Mom kept insisting, so she started doing the dishes. I said, "Mom, just leave them alone." But she wouldn't, and it was upsetting me. She wasn't relaxing and leaving me and my house as we wanted it to be. I begin to feel: "This is my house. This is my job. I should be doing those dishes, but I don't want to until my friends leave."

Marie: Why didn't you say something?

Charles: (to Marie) Excuse me, what word did you use?

Marie: Oh. (to Karen) How is it possible you didn't say something?

Karen: Maybe I thought I did.

Charles: Karen Anne!

Karen: Yes.

Charles: How is it possible you allow your mother to place you in that type of state? Are you looking at all your options?

Karen: I could have gotten up and just physically moved her away from the sink and sat her down or given her something else to do to distract her from wanting to be the mother.

Charles: Would it be possible for you to quietly say, "Mother, this is my house. I would be far more comfortable if you sat down now?"

Karen: I could do that.

Charles: Good, and would that be Karen as opposed to Karen Anne?

Karen: Yes.

Charles: Is it possible you would like to allow Karen to have some strength within the relationship with your parents?

Karen: Yes, especially when it comes down to the Karen Anne feelings. When I feel Karen Anne coming on, I want to say things Karen doesn't feel.

Charles: Right. Karen Anne still has the feelings of a child. Mind you, those feelings are all right. They simply come from the past, when they were all you knew. Is this correct?

Karen: Yes. It has a lot to do with Karen and Mother and Father. It discourages me that I can't seem to break out of the Karen Anne feeling.

Charles: There's nothing wrong with those feelings. They were the feeling Karen Anne had. However, we might choose to explore how it's possible these feelings still have so much strength in the present moment.

Karen: I'm game. I don't like it when it happens.

Charles: Was Karen Anne always there from the time you were a small child?

Karen: Yes, but I don't remember how far back.

Charles: Karen Anne knows how far back.

Karen: Probably.

Charles: So, Karen Anne, how far back do you go? (to class) Watch here as we talk. Watch her body. You'll see a lot of changes take place.

Karen: Karen Anne needs help to get back.

Charles: Karen Anne, how old are you?

Karen: 17.

Charles: Okay, you are Karen Anne, and you are 17 years old. What are you doing?

Karen: Not what my parents want me to do.

Charles: What are you doing? Are you in high school?

Karen: Yes.

Charles: Do you have a boyfriend?

Karen: Yes.

Charles: Do your parents like your boyfriend?

Karen: Yes. Actually, he's a lot older than I am, so they don't really like that very much.

Charles: They don't like the fact he's older than you?

Karen: He had an apartment, and they don't like that.

Charles: Hey, we all know what happens with people who have their own apartments.

Karen: They don't like that, either. (everybody laughs)

Charles: It's okay. Things happen. Life happens live and you're there. Karen Anne at 17, can you remember Karen Anne at 16?

Karen: Yes.

Charles: Okay, so be 16.

Karen: Okay.

Charles: You're 16 years old now?

Karen: Yes.

Charles: What's going on?

Karen: I've got my own car, and I can do whatever I want because I have my own car. And I have freedom. Karen Anne's fighting back. She's getting out, breaking out.

Charles: Wait a minute, who's talking to me?

Karen: I am. Karen's talking.

Charles: I thought so.

Karen: I'm getting out. I'm rebelling for all I couldn't do when I was younger.

Charles: (to class) Did you notice the voice change when she went from Karen Anne to Karen? When you're working like this, you need to pay very close attention to who you are talking with because there are voice differences based on age. Due to that and the language pattern change, I knew I was talking to Karen rather than Karen Anne. (to Karen) I want Karen Anne back, please.

Karen: Okay.

Charles: You've got your own car?

Karen: Yes.

Charles: Do you have a boyfriend?

Karen: No, not really.

Charles: You meet the older guy when you're 17?

Karen: Yes.

Charles: Is there anything in particular going on? Is there any big source of conflict between you and your parents?

Karen: Only my wanting to do what I want to do when I want to do it.

Charles: You're a willful child, are you?

Karen: Yes, I remember there was this really bad storm, and I wanted to go to see somebody, a boyfriend.

Charles: Who's talking?

Karen: Karen. (voice changes) I couldn't go see him because my car was frozen shut, but I still wanted to go. I sat out there for hours and chipped ice off my car. Then the Governor closed all the roads due to the weather. I still wanted to go. I was gonna go, but I couldn't get my car door open.

Charles: Okay, and Karen Anne at 16, do you remember Karen Anne at 15?

Karen: Yes. I was a sophomore in high school, and I started smoking pot. It was the first time I tried pot. It was fun!!

Charles: Something forbidden.

Karen: Yes. I'd never get stoned. I'd just smoke it.

Charles: Fine, and Karen Anne at 15, do you remember Karen Anne at 14?

Karen: Yeah, 14 was . . .

Charles: A freshman?

Karen: No, 14 was in 8th grade.

Charles: Wait, if 15 is a sophomore in high school, how can you be in 8th grade rather than a freshman?

Karen: I was both. Different school years.

Charles: And just a peon. What's happening?

Karen: Not much. Just girlfriends.

Charles: No boyfriend?

Karen: No, 13 had a boyfriend.

Charles: 13 had a boyfriend? Let's go to 13. Having a boyfriend is much more fun than having a bunch of girl friends, isn't it?

Karen: Yeah, really.

Charles: Is he older?

Karen: No, he's in my math class.

Charles: Does he like you?

Karen: Yeah, he likes me. The girls all want to beat me up because he likes me.

Charles: How's your relationship with your parents?

Karen: Secretive.

Charles: On whose part, yours or theirs?

Karen: Mine.

Charles: How is it possible you're being secretive with, and around, your parents.

Karen: Because I have my own room, and I'm learning a lot about myself. I don't want to tell them things so I withdraw into myself.

Charles: Were you withdrawn at 12?

Karen: 12 was when I got in trouble for drinking. I ended up in the hospital, and my mother sat up with me all night. When I woke up, the first thing I said was, "Am I in trouble?" But they didn't know what was wrong with me. They just knew I was at a dance and I got real, real sick and was taken to the hospital.

Charles: You were drinking?

Karen: Yes, I was angry and depressed.

Charles: What were you angry and depressed about?

Karen: I'm not sure. There's this fear.

Charles: Are you angry and depressed because of this fear?

Karen: Yes, I think so.

Charles: What are you afraid of?

Karen: I don't know.

Charles: Okay, well, Karen Anne at 12, do you remember Karen Anne at 11?

Karen: I don't remember 11. And 10 is just bits and pieces, not as clearly as I can remember year by year before that. I remember getting stung, not getting stung by a bee, but getting upset when a bee flew in my ear at a party. I thought I was more like 4 years old because I was so little then. It flew in my ear, and no one would believe me. I was shaking my head. It hurt so bad, and I was screaming, and my dad came in the house. He jumped up. We have stairs going from the basement to the attic. My brother saw him, and Dad made it up the stairs in three steps because he was running to see what the problem was. He got a flashlight, looked in my ear, found the bug, and pulled it out.

Charles: So you remember 4 or 5 real well.

Karen: Yeah, I remember going to school. I remember the first day of school real well.

Charles: And you can remember 12, but you can't remember 11?

Karen: I remember third grade.

Charles: You can remember 12, and you're having trouble with remembering 11?

Karen: Yeah.

Charles: Do you remember your 12th birthday?

Karen: I remember my 13th birthday.

Charles: You remember your 13th birthday?

Karen: Yeah. Well, maybe I remember my 12th birthday. I was in Florida for 12 or 13 because we took the train with my grandmother. We celebrate either my 12th or 13th birthday in Florida.

Charles: Okay, great. Now I want you to jump. I want you to go back to Karen Anne at 8. Karen Anne at 12, do you remember Karen Anne at 8? That would be third grade.

Karen: Yeah, I remember third grade.

Charles: And what's going on with your parents?

Karen: Dad was working. I guess nights still. He was a policeman until I was 10 or 11.

Charles: Your father was a policeman until you were 10 or 11?

Karen: Yes.

Charles: Does your mother worry about him coming home?

Karen: Yes.

Charles: Do you feel her concern?

Karen: (starts to cry) He worked until midnight.

Charles: And you don't get to sleep until midnight, until Daddy comes home, do you? (Karen is crying hard) You're worried about Daddy.

Karen: Oh yes. Oh, Daddy, please come home.

Charles: Karen, come out, come back to the present. It's okay. Now we have found out how it's possible you can't access 10 or 11. We found out what you're afraid of. 10 and 11 have anxiety complexes about Daddy and his safety.

Karen: He would come home and tuck me in.

Charles: That's how you would know Daddy was okay.

Karen: Yes.

Charles: Let it go. Come back to the present moment. You know your father is active and well today. You can let go of all that old fear.

Karen: Yes.

Charles: Then understand the message from the past and let go of the worry and rebellion and fear which came from your concerns at that past moment in time.

As we can see from this example, the basis of the Behavior Karen was enacting as an adult stemmed from a childhood fear that her father would not return home in the evening because he was a policeman and might be killed. This is true of so many of the Behaviors we have as adults, and like Karen, most of us are unaware of where either our Beliefs or our Behavior come from. Unless we are willing to examine where our Behaviors come from, change and growth as an individual is almost impossible.

One of the important things to remember is that we do not assign a negative value to the original context of the Belief and Behavior. It is what allowed us to survive then. It is the by-product of whatever was occurring at that moment in time. And it may be almost totally counter-productive in the NOW moment, for who and what we choose to Be presently.

6

The Bottom Line
(My Story)

WHENEVER I GIVE A WORKSHOP, somebody usually asks, "Charles, what you say is really interesting, and I'd really like to believe what you're saying, but does it work?"

In order to answer this question, I would like to share the story of my father's and my relationship.

My father was something else. As far as I knew as I was growing up, I would never be able to do anything which would please him; I would never be good enough for him. I had received this message the whole time I was growing up. Nothing I ever did was correct, or good enough. I knew this. I lived with it. It was the Reality of my world.

Now, my father was raised by his father. Grandpa Frost was born in the 1880s in rural, agricultural America. He, in turn, was raised by his father, my great grandfather, in even more rural, agricultural America. It was an America in which the whole family worked together on the family farm, or in the family business. Those who had no such prospects, left home at an early age to be trained in some profession. A sixth-grade education was a good education for most people. The children worked with the rest of the family all day long. By the time it came to dinner, there was no need for the children to talk about what had happened to them during the day. Everybody was there and already knew what had happened. And even if that was not so, a child was supposed to be seen and not heard.

By the time my father was being raised in the 1920s and 1930s, this was no longer true, and by the time he raised his family in the 1950s and 1960s, it was well over a hundred years later. America was an urban, industrial nation, and it was a whole different world than when my great-grandfather was being raised.

People were being treated certain ways because this is the way people are treated, and the boneless ham principle of life was busy at work. As with most homes, the reason behind something which had become a family tradition had been lost. Things were being done a certain way because it was the way "things have always been done."

My father had been treated a certain way when he was growing up and this reflected in how he treated other people in general, not just his children. In his view of the world, he was being kind and loving when he "kept control" at the dinner table. He thought it was the way it was supposed to be done; after all, it had been done to him. He did not set out to intentionally psychologically and emotionally abuse his seven chidden, and that is exactly what he did. Yet, he was doing the very best he knew how to do with the skills, abilities, and resources he had available to him, his knowledge of them, and his opportunity to use them.

And the message I kept receiving was that I was "not good enough." Being told I was "not of general interest" when I had something to say at dinner was only a part of this message. When I was 12 years old, I decide to quit playing football. At that point in my life, I was small for my age, weighing 98 pounds in full equipment, and I was not very well coordinated. The upper weight limit for the league I was playing in was 145 pounds plus equipment. I was playing against boys who weighed 150 pounds or more in their equipment and who were far more coordinated than I was. In short, I was getting killed out there. One day, as I got up from the bottom of a pile, I made what seemed to be a very good decision to me. I quit. I went up to the coach and said, "Coach, I quit."

He said, "Okay, Frost, go home."

I got home at 6:30 PM rather than the usual 7:00 PM, and my father asked me how come I was home so early. I told him I had quit, and he said, "You're a sissy, and nobody will like you."

Once again, my experience of myself had just been invalidated. I did not want to be a sissy. I wanted people to like me. I played football for two more years, spending most of my time either face down in the dirt or riding the bench. After that, I never played football again.

In 1968, I was within two weeks of getting my Master's Degree in American History, three weeks of starting to teach high school, and I was having dinner with my parents. George Wallace was running for President of the United States and doing very well in the polls. Some polls showed Nixon, Humphrey, and Wallace each with about 30% of the vote. Dad and I got into a conversation regarding Wallace, the Electorial College, and third patty candidates. He remarked that Wallace might throw the election into the House of Representatives by breaking all of Teddy Roosevelt's third party records set in 1912 when he ran as a Bull Moose. I looked up and told him that if he was referring to the percentage of vote, he was correct, Teddy held that record; and, if he was referring to electorial vote, he was correct, Teddy held that record; however, if he was referring to the total number of votes received, that record was held by Senator Robert LaFollette of Wisconsin when he ran as a Progressive in 1924.

"You're wrong."

"No, Dad, this is correct. There were more than twice as many people voting in 1924 than there were in 1912, and LaFollette pulled almost 1,000,000 more votes than Teddy had gotten 12 years earlier."

"You're wrong"

"Dad. . . ."

"I'll bet you a thousand dollars you're wrong."

"Dad, I don't have a thousand dollars, and I don't want to bet you."

"Put up or shut up, wise guy!"

"Dad, please. . . ."

"Put up or shut up!!"

I got up from the table, went down to the basement, got an American History book, went back upstairs, and laid it down in front of my Dad. He looked at it, and then turned to me and said, "If you had been sure, you would have bet me."

What happened?

I was right, I had the correct information, and it still was not good enough.

Perhaps the best conversation about the on-going "not good enough" message I received all my life took place in a class I was teaching.

Charles: You might want to take a look at your relationship with your parents. This is one of the "World View" shapers. When we were young, our parents seemed so old and very wise; then, as we reach the age they were, we begin to realize how many doubts and fears we have, and that they must have had doubts and fears also. While this knowledge does us a great deal of good in the present moment, it does not change the Experience of that younger Self unless we take the Knowledge back to it. You see, one of the main reasons most small children think their parents are so perfect is that they are so physically small compared to their parents. The child feels towered over. If you are going to work with a child, make sure to get down to their size level and make direct eye contact. This allows them to feel far more responsive, far more trusted. This is important because the normal message most children get is that they are small and insignificant. This is the message which is continually given to them. And, until we can get in touch with the "child" inside each of us, the "child" will continue to have those feelings. We need to let it know that what it feels, and how it feels it, are all right. When this happens, the "child within" can begin to feel a lot of relief as we stop blaming it and take the responsibility for our own "grown-up" lives. Until we do this, we continue to act out of whatever impressions we had when we were young.

Diane: Like losing my temper, that's my child coming out.

Charles: Right. We are dealing with the parts of Self and must address them if we are to make changes and grow. Increasingly, as we go along in this class, we are going to talk about not only the generalized Behavior we currently exhibit, but what past Perceptions control an activity or an emotion.

For example, there was a point about a year after my divorce when I started to date again. All of a sudden, I found something was not congruent. I started to check my internal reference points and found, much to my horror, that my social director was a 17-year-old Part of Self who had never been on a date. Now, that's not necessarily bad, if you can live with it; however, a 43-year-old man who had been married for 11 years doesn't really need a 17-year-old social director who hasn't been on a date. Look at how incongruent that is. Still, it had never been an issue in the marriage or during the course of the total relationship of 15 years. Thus, the last social contacts were years before, and we are now dealing with somebody who is in their mid-20s. Yes, there is still an exponential gap between a 26-year-old and a 17-year-old social director, but it is not quite as incongruent as with somebody who is 43. Discovering this gap also explained to me how it was possible so many of the relationships I had prior to my former wife had not worked out.

We want to remember a Filter is how we view something. A Filter, particularly an old Filter, comes from what we were, and where we were at that moment in time. It may not be appropriate in the present context, so we have to address how we got that viewpoint originally. We have to address how we got that Filter, what the Belief System is, and what the secondary gain is. Then, and at only then, can we begin to address the issue of change.

Now, my 17-year-old is basing its view of Reality on what was occurring at that time. For me, at 43, 26 years later, to have the same view of Reality is insane, and very, very nonproductive.

Think of the number of people you know who say: "It was this way last week, last month, last year, ten years ago, therefore, it always has to be this way." We are taking an old script, an old Filter, something from back there in the Past, and applying it as FOREVER. Under such a framework, there is no possibility of change and growth.

Change and growth do not have to mean destruction. This is what a lot of people feel about growth and change: "If I change and grow, so-and-so won't love me any more." This isn't necessarily so. Every human being is growing and changing, even if they are choosing not to. The choice to not grow and change is a choice, and that is a type of growth, too, because it means the person will progressively get more and more rigid and narrow in their view of life. And if the significant other is expanding while you are contracting, what's going to happen?

Patti: Ones going to overtake the other.

Charles: Right. There's going to be conflict. Yet, if both people are expanding, they may find new ways in which they can enjoy each other. So, growth and change are expansion. The decision not to change and grow means there will be contraction. If you are continually contacting, then there is less and less common ground. The narrower the scope, the less we have to share. Therefore, change and growth are positives because they give us more to share.

Diane: What happened to your 17-year-old?

Charles: My 17-year-old. I started to write poetry at the age of 16, and the first poem I wrote I don't want to get into. I mean, one of the very first poems started:

> I love you, I love you, I love you.
> I know it sounds fantastic,
> Or maybe even drastic,
> But it's true,
> I love you.

We are not talking great poetry here.

Patti: That was pretty romantic for a 16-year-old. I mean, most guys are not on that level. It's like, oh no, not the L word!!!

Charles: Yes, that's true, most men can't say the L word at any age. "What do you mean you want to hear the L word? I know the F word real good, but not the L word."

Judy: They are afraid of the C word, too.

Charles: Yes, Commitment. And we need to get back to our discussion of Filters. Now, the Experiential Framework of a Part stops at the point when it becomes a Part. It still can see what happens later on, but those events are not really a part of its experience. I couldn't tell my internal 17-year-old to stop being 17 or that his experiences were invalid. Instead, I spoke to him in such a manner that I was able to take control of my social life.

Patti: How did you do that?

Charles: It went something like: You know, it's really great you've taken care of social activities all these years. Nobody else seemed to want the job, and I really appreciate the job you've done. And, under the present circumstances, I know I am not 17 years old any longer. I have had a lifetime of experiences I would like to incorporate into how I relate to people. It might be of more value to us as a congruent whole to allow the present Self be in charge of these interactions and use the knowledge it has. Still, you've been really creative to be in charge for so long, and you found some pretty creative ways to interact with other people, even if some of those ways were inappropriate for the present moment. How would you feel about going over in the Creative area and helping us out when we want to write poetry or short stories? You could be a really big asset over in Creative.

Please notice, I never attacked my 17-year-old. It always did the best it knew how to do.

· Judy: How did you identify it was your 17-year-old running your social life?

Charles: It hadn't been on a date. That was one clue. The first time I went on an actual date was after my 17th birthday. I also based the conclusion on some other Behaviors. For example, if I was just out with friends, or went out with a person I wasn't romantically interested in, the context was different and I acted more mature.

Patti: So your Behavior was different on a date. Did you want to sit in the car and drink beer, or what? Help me understand.

Robert: What would a 17-year-old do out on a date with a 40-year-old woman? (everybody laughs)

Charles: Well, not necessarily just that. There are all types of inappropriate Behaviors. A 17-year-old can be very over-whelming sometimes in stating his likes and dislikes. I would be out with somebody and found myself saying, "I want you to know I'm really, really interested in you." That was 17, not 43, and the reaction I got was "What the Hell? Get away from me, you Bozo. I want to ship you off to another state, and that still might be too close." When I recognized this was going on I asked myself where my Behavior was coming from and I recognized it as my 17-year-old.

Other factors were able to play into that. For example, another Filter of the 17-year-old has to do with the matter of sex. If I went out with you 3 or 4 times, you'd expect me to at least try and kiss you good night, right?

Diane: Right.

Charles: I wasn't. Here's how that was possible. My dad's sum total of sex eduction to me as a young man was: "Son, if you ever go out on a date, always treat the girl the same way you would treat your mother or your sisters. Don't ever do anything you wouldn't do with your mother or sisters."

Now, my dad did the best he knew how to do. He did the best he could with the resources he had. I recognize this, yet I heard that speech from the time I was 13 years old, and it became very ingrained. What would this do for the quality of any future interactions? If you begin to have a physical reaction, what happens? You have this person tapping you on your shoulder, emotionally, and saying, "You're not suppose to feel that! This isn't something you'd do with your mother or your sisters."

And I found this was still in place. The reactions would still arise. There was still this tremendous avoidance/approach pattern to all of my relationships. "I want a kiss—no, I don't—yes, I do—no, I don't." And the loop could go on endlessly and the Behavior exhibited as a result could get really weird.

After that, I found several more Filters which were no longer productive. I had a 6-year-old who would come to the dinner table to talk about what had happened during the day, and my father would .say, "Not of general interest." This meant the subject could no longer be discussed. Thus, at a very early age, I learned that what I had to say, what I felt, and what I did were not important to the significant adults in my life.

And my 12-year-old was told he was a sissy because he didn't want to play football any more. He didn't want to hit and be hit. My father told me I was a sissy and I was letting my friends down by not playing. I wasn't allowed to quit. Once again, my feelings were invalidated by the most significant adult in my world.

All of these are Perceptual Filters. They come from the past and past experiences. Once we recognize what is going on, we can go inside and work on it. The present doesn't have to be the same as the past. We can change our Perceptions, and, therefore, we can change what we Believe and how we choose to act and react. Each of us is responsible for ourselves.

Bonnie: Have you ever called your dad and told him some of the things you've discovered?

Charles: To what purpose? I've worked through it. And I recognize my dad did the very best he could. For me to hold him guilty for that, or to hold any resentment against him for doing his best, is really very counter-productive. If I do that I'm assigning blame and guilt, and I haven't really let go of the past. If I do that, I'm still trapped back there. Thus, I merely accept my father for who and what he is, and was, and know he did the best he knew how to do with the skills, abilities, and resources he had available to him at the time, and I move on with my own life!!!

Or so I thought. That was October, 1988, and, then, in May, 1989, I was on the phone with my mother late one afternoon. At the end of the conversation, she said, "Oh, by the way, dear, your father was at the doctor's last week, and they've given him six months to live."

When the call ended, I got up from my desk, closed the door to my office, and sat down and cried, and cried, and cried. I was crying not only because of the shock I felt a and because I was starting the grief process early to avoid the rush, I was crying because I was ANGRY!!! I was angry because my father was going to die. My father was going to die without ever acknowledging me as a person, without ever telling me that I had done something right!! How very inconsiderate of him!!! How dare he die before he has acknowledged my worthiness as a human being? How dare he?

This was all extremely external. My sense of Self-Worth was tied up outside of myself. My father (an external) had never acknowledged me (externally) so that I could be all right as an individual (internally). There was no way I could ever "win" in this situation, so I cried, and I cried, and I cried.

Understand the time frame on this. This is 2 years after my divorce. It is 14 months after I received certification in N.L.P. It is 13 months after I was asked to first do some counselling/frameworking for/with other people. It is 11 months after I taught my first classes on my theories of Change and Growth. It is 4 months after my first workshop. And I am sitting there, crying, because my father has not acknowledged me as an individual.

I knew I had to do something, and I did not know what.

In August, 1989, I rented a cottage 35 mites outside of Grand Rapids for 2 weeks. It was the first time I had been in Michigan in 2 years. I had been there the August after the divorce. My father did not travel well, so I could go up to Grand Rapids and see him and my mother as well as visit with friends and go fishing.

The first night I was back, I drove up to have dinner with my parents. As we started dinner, I was greeted by my father's warm welcome: "Chuck, tell me about this Unity thing!"

I had joined the Unity Church in the 2 years since my last visit, and he did not know anything about it and wanted to know what it was. This was dangerous ground for me. This was an opinion question. I was 43 years old and could not ever remember my father asking me an opinion question. Further, I could remember all too well what had happened the last time I had given an opinion back in 1968. Still, I proceeded to answer him, telling him how New Thought Christianity not only looked at God's Love as an external, but that God was within each of us, and that God's Love was thus present within the life of each of us at every moment of time, that there was no separation from God. I made some references to Jeffersonian dualism, Emerson's Oversoul', and the ancient Greeks, and kept it all under 5 minutes. I knew that anything long would be cut off.

He looked across the table at me and said, "Well, that makes sense."

I was surprised by his answer. I also knew his answer meant the conversation was over, but I did not let it end there. I looked at him and said, "Dad, I want you to know that I love you and I accept you for who, and what, you are."

He looked at me blankly for a second and then responded, "Well that's good, because I'm not gonna change."

He had missed the point, hadn't he? He did not understand what I was saying, did he?

No, he did not. And it did not really matter, because at that moment in time, if I really meant what I had just said, I was no longer waiting for him to accept me as an individual (external) so that I could be all right (internal), and then, maybe, I could love and accept him. If I meant what I had just said, I had moved within to that place of Self-Love within (remember—"Love thy neighbour AS thyself") and was able to extend it outward to where he was. It did not matter if he understood what I was saying, he got the meaning perfectly well.

Please notice, I did not say how he had treated me and my 6 brothers and sisters was appropriate or productive. I simply told him I Loved him and accepted him as he was.

Over the next 2 weeks, I had dinner with them several times as well as seeing old friends and doing some fishing. Then, on the Saturday before Labor Day, I had lunch with them after checking out of the cottage. After lunch, we hugged and kissed and said our good-byes. I got to the front door of their apartment. I was loaded down with presents from my 44th birthday and a "goodie" basket for the 20-hour drive back to Dallas. As I stood there, suddenly it hit me: "He's going to die. I'm never going to see him alive again. Have I said everything I want to say to him?"

And I knew I had not. And I dropped everything, and I turned, and I hugged him one more time, kissed him on the cheek, and whispered in his ear, "I Love you, you old bear. Thank you and good-bye."

And I left knowing I would never see my father alive again.

My parents 50th wedding anniversary was in October, 1990. Dad had been planning it for years. He was not going to miss it. He rallied.

And in July, 1990, I arrived in Grand Rapids, having closed my sales business to begin going around the country doing workshops and seminars for a living. I stopped in Grand Rapids on my way to The Great Lakes Unity Lay Person's Retreat where I was one of the speakers. I was having lunch with them because lunch was now his best time of day, and I was greeted by his warm welcome: "Chuck! How come you closed a perfectly good sales business to go out travelling around the country in your car, doing workshops and seminars, living like a gypsy on the fringes of society?"

I responded, "Because it's fun."

The conversation died for lack of a common reference point.

In August, we had a big party at my brother's place 40 miles north of Grand Rapids. It included everyone: all my brothers and sisters, their children, the spouses of those who were still married, my uncle and his family, close family friends. It was quite a party. Still, we were going to have a private party for just my parents and the 7 of us on their anniversary in late October.

By late September, it became clear that some of my brothers and sisters were planning not to attend the second party. They had quietly let my mother know they would not be coming and that they would show him what they thought about the way he had treated them when they were growing up.

My mother was distressed by this, and shared her distress with me. In early October, I wrote a 7-page letter to my brothers and sisters. The first page ended with: "You know, we grew up in a dysfunctional home. Oops! We're not supposed to talk about such things. Read on."

The key page was the fourth page as I shared with them something which had happened.

I got to Dad-sit about 10 days ago. Mom had some things she had to do, and Dad can't be left alone, so I Dad-sat.

Dad decided this would be a nice time for he and I to talk. You all know this one. The conversation followed the all too familiar pattern: he talked, I listened. And, yes, he told me how to run my life, what I was doing wrong, how insufficient I was as a person—and more than that, he talked at length about the past and trying to do what was right, trying to show Love. He spoke of his father, and his grandfather, and how "tough" they were. He told of times of loneliness and isolation in his past and how very alone he felt. I could feel his awareness of death and his almost desperate efforts to "sort out" and "make peace" with his past, with who, and what, he is, and what he has done with his life. He feels the pain of that which he wanted to achieve and did not. And I listened without correcting, or adding, or even feeling resentment for the fact he doesn't have a clue about who, or what I am. I only felt Love and Compassion for another human being who was reaching out in the only way he knew how, who was asking for Love and Understanding with words unspoken, praying for Redemption and Forgiveness from things done, and things left undone.

When he was done, I just reached over, hugged him, and said, "I Love you, Dad."

He cried.

I was 45 years old and had never seen my father cry before. Then, he stiffened up, and was the tough old bird I had always known.

We had a very successful anniversary party, and I left Grand Rapids in late October, 1990, knowing I would never see my father alive again. He was slipping. All of us could see the difference between mid-August and late October. The next time we would be together would be his funeral at some point over the winter.

Dad loved Christmas. He rallied.

And in early January, 1991, he and my mom sent out a joint letter to their children. There was a copy of a Living Will stating he did not want any heroic measures taken to extend his life if it came to that.

In his part of the letter, he explained his desire not to drain the resources he and Mom had spent a lifetime working to establish. He said he considered Life to be more of a "Quality" thing than a "Quantity" thing, and that he considered death as a natural extension of life.

Until that moment in time, I had not known how much alike my father and I thought.

He also asked us not to "grive" his passing as he had lived his life his way. I thought about that, and then wrote back several weeks later, saying, in part:

"If I grive anything, Dad, it's the time lost over the years spent in not understanding. I spent so much of my Life waiting for you to change so that I could be happy, so that I could feel that you accepted me. That was most unkind. I made you responsible for my happiness, and that was never true. What had to change was my attitude. Not you in any way.

Just me.

Just my attitude."

And I arrived in Grand Rapids, Memorial Day weekend, 1991. Breakfast was now my father's best time of day, and it was not so good. And at that first breakfast, I was greeted by my father's warm welcome: "Chuck! Are you making it financially?"

"Yeah, Dad, I'm okay financially. I don't make what I did in the sales business, not even close, and I'm doing all right. I have the money to get from one place to the next and to pay the bills back in Dallas. Yeah, Dad. I'm okay financially."

Nothing more was said, and I spent the summer coming and going as I did workshops throughout the Midwest. I had rented an apartment with a good friend, and would see my parents several times a week, often "Dad-sitting" so my Mom could go do other things.

In late August, a few days after my 46th birthday, I was once again "Dad-sitting." We were talking about the changes which were taking place in eastern Europe and how they would affect the rest of the world, and, sure enough, about 9:30 AM, he fell asleep in mid-sentence. He was so very weak.

I picked up *The Wall Street Journal* from the table next to his chair and sat across from him reading. He would sleep for the rest of the morning, waking up when Mom came home to fix lunch. As I was sitting there reading, suddenly I heard, "Chuck."

I had never heard that tone of voice from my father before and I dropped the paper. He was leaning forward in his chair. I begin to think: "Okay, there's hot water on the stove for tea in case he's congested, his inhaler is next to that, his oxygen tank is in his bedroom, his insulin is in the refrigerator, and I know where his heart medicine is. And I know how to dial 911."

"Yeah, Pop."

Very slowly he asked, "Are—you—happy?"

I was floored. It had never occurred to me that it mattered one bit to him if I was happy. I responded, "Yeah, Dad, I'm happy. I'm leading my Life, my way, doing the very best I know how to with the skills, abilities, and resources I have available to me and my opportunity to use them. I know I'm not the man you would have had me be. I never could be. I always had to be me. Yeah, Dad, I'm happy. I'm as happy as I know how to Be."

"That's good." And he went back to steep.

Two days later, I left Grand Rapids to do workshops in Atlanta, then working my way across the nation, where ten weeks later, when I was in Ashland, Oregon, I received word that my father had died at the age of 74.

My friends, we do not ever get to "Are you happy?" without first going through "I Love you and I accept you for who and what you are" two years earlier. You see, what was "normal" for my father and I was to argue and fight with each other, and without a Perceptual Shift on my part, we will spend the last 2 years of his life doing what he had done with the first 44 of mine, which was argue and fight. One Perceptual Shift made all the difference.

The week before he died, I wrote in my journal:

"Redemption.

Ultimately, I believe each of us seeks Redemption. We seek to redeem ourselves within the framework of Life. We strive to achieve a sort of Self-Knowledge that when we face God, we will have something to show for our lives.

Each of us seeks Redemption from past sin, from those things done, and those things left undone. We seek the assurance that our individual Life amounted to some-thing—somehow, some way.

And we feel the futility of it all.

Dad is dying. I feel him slipping away. And he no longer thinks of the hopes and dreams he once had; rather, he focuses on the Love he has felt. The Love he tried to give, and the Love given and received.

Love extended.

Love denied.

And the final Redemption is Love, given freely, openly, without conditions.

Just Love.

And Redemption.

Redemption, then, is based on the Love and Acceptance we extend to ourselves. Redemption comes from Self-Acceptance, regardless of past sin or present condition.

Love.   Redemption.

Thus, Life is about embracing our humanity, not denying it, not beating up on ourselves for what we have done, or not done; rather it is accepting and embracing the fullness of ourselves and each other.

No expectations.

Just accepting,

embracing,

Loving,

and redeeming."

I believe that all of Life is Love expressing, and that all of Life is merely the opportunity to learn to Love more. That is all there is, Love, and the opportunity to express Love.

Just Love.

And I would like to close this book with the poem I wrote for the first group of students I had in 1988. I was so touched by the changes I saw them making in their lives that one Sunday afternoon after they left, I wrote:

Love Is
even as you are
and I am,
and is not
dependent
upon us
for its existence.

It merely Is,
and if we,
each of us,
collectively,
and
individually,
will let go
of our doubts,
and fears,
and expectations,
of each other,
and ourselves,
then
we
can
find
the Love
we have always sought;
springing,
not from without,
but from within,
then
radiating outward,
and coming back to us,
for we can never get,
what we cannot give,
and with,
or without us,
Love Is.

For information on workshops and seminars conducted by
Charles Frost, please write:

Charles Frost
P.O. Box 142254
Irving, TX 75014-2254